BAD SEED

BAD SEED

A play in two acts

B Y

MAXWELL ANDERSON

The dramatization of William March's novel

THE BAD SEED

This is an Anderson House book

DODD, MEAD & COMPANY · NEW YORK

PS
3505
A53157
B36

Copyright, © 1955 by MAXWELL ANDERSON

NOTE

CAUTION: Professionals and amateurs are hereby warned that BAD SEED, being fully protected under the Copyright Laws of the United States of America, the British Empire, including the Dominion of Canada, and all other countries of the Copyright Union, is subject to royalty. All rights, including professional, amateur, motion picture, recitation, lecturing, public reading, radio broadcasting, television and the rights of translation in foreign languages are strictly reserved. Particular emphasis is laid on the question of readings, permission for which must be secured from the author's agent, in writing. All inquiries should be addressed to the author's agent, Harold Freedman, 101 Park Avenue, New York City.

Published March 1955
Second printing April 1955

Printed in the United States of America
by Vail-Ballou Press, Inc., Binghamton, N. Y.

Library of Congress Catalog Card Number: 55-7822

BAD SEED had its first performance in New York at the Forty-sixth Street Theatre December 8, 1954, when the play was produced by The Playwrights' Company, Inc., with the following cast:

Rhoda Penmark...............Patty McCormack
Col. Kenneth Penmark ....John O'Hare
Christine Penmark...................Nancy Kelly
Monica Breedlove.................Evelyn Varden
Emory Wages....................Joseph Holland
Leroy...........................Henry Jones
Miss Fern.......................Joan Croydon
Reginald Tasker ....Lloyd Gough
Mrs. Daigle.....................Eileen Heckart
Mr. Daigle....................Wells Richardson
Messenger........................George Gino
Richard Bravo ....Thomas Chalmers

48999

BAD SEED

Act One

SCENE 1

*The one set is the apartment of Colonel and Mrs. Penmark, in a suburb
of a southern city. We see a tastefully furnished living room, with colonial pieces and reproductions, expensive but not too gaudy. The pictures on the walls are views of New York City in the early nineteenth
century. The door to the front hall is at stage left, the door to an inner
hallway at stage right, a door to the kitchen—which is partially visible
—is at right rear, a door to a den containing a piano is at left rear.
Large windows with heavy drapes flood the room with early morning
light. There is a dining table at the bay window with chairs about it,
a couch at the left with a coffee table near by. There are two or three
easy chairs in a semi-circle facing the coffee table. A rug on the floor
is vari-colored rag colonial.*

*Rhoda Penmark, a neat, quaint and pretty little girl of eight, sits, seri-
ously reading a book, on the chair right. She turns a page carefully,
absorbed in the story. Colonel Kenneth Penmark, a good-looking
officer of thirty-five or so, comes in from the right, carrying two fairly
new suitcases. He sets them down near the outer door and turns,
seeing Rhoda.*

KENNETH   Why, 'morning, Rhoda! Up, and dressed and ready for
the day! Wearing your best perfume?

1

RHODA   [*Marking her place*] Yes, I am, daddy.

KENNETH   That's right, this is the day of the picnic. I hope there's
            a breeze off the water.

RHODA   Miss Fern says there always is.

KENNETH   She says it never rains on the first of June, too. Don't
            count on it.

RHODA   Are you leaving today, daddy?

KENNETH   My plane goes in an hour. Back to Washington and the
            Pentagon and a climate that coddles eggs.

RHODA   I like coddled eggs.

KENNETH   You like everything. You're just too good to be true.

            [*He pulls her braids, and she smiles up at him*]

RHODA   How long will you be gone?

KENNETH   Sealed orders, darling. All I know is I'll be home as soon
            as I can. What will you give me if I give you a basket of
            kisses?

RHODA   I'll give you a basket of hugs.

            [*He leans down to hug and kiss her*]

KENNETH   I like your hugs.

RHODA   I like your kisses, daddikins! You're so big and strong!

KENNETH   I'll miss you. The General doesn't have one pretty girl on
            his whole staff!

RHODA   I wish he didn't have my daddy! I'll miss you every day!

KENNETH   Will you write to me?

RHODA   Do you want me to?

KENNETH   Of course I want you to.

RHODA   Then I'll write to you every day.

KENNETH   Every time I write to mother I'll put in a note for you!

RHODA   Will you really?

KENNETH   Really and truly. And every time the General tells a good
             joke I'll send you an official report!

RHODA   Oh, daddy, that won't be very often! You'd better send
             me the bad ones too!

KENNETH   Sweetheart, I will!
             [MRS. PENMARK *comes in from the den in a becoming
             morning gown. She is somewhat under thirty, a very
             pretty, gentle and gracious woman, quite obviously dedi-
             cated to her husband and child. The kind of woman
             whose life is given meaning by the affection she gives and
             receives*]
             I shall write daily to both my sweethearts unless some-
             body makes a mistake and starts a shooting war and we
             all have to go underground.

             [*He kisses Christine, his wife, who has brought his
             briefcase and goes into his arms without a word. They
             have said goodbye previously, but she can't let him go
             without another embrace*]

RHODA   Would you go underground if there was a war?

KENNETH   Yes, I would, and, by gum, I'd go fast!

RHODA   You said "by gum" because I was here.

KENNETH   That's right, I did.

CHRISTINE   Take care.

KENNETH   I will. I'll wire you the minute we're on the ground. Take
              care of each other, you two.

CHRISTINE   We will.
              [*The doorbell rings a delicate little chime*]
              That's Monica and Emory. They wanted to say a last
              goodbye to you.

KENNETH   Oh.

              [*He goes to the door. Meanwhile* CHRISTINE *looks at
              Rhoda's hair*]

RHODA   Is it all right?

CHRISTINE   It's perfect, darling, braids and all.

KENNETH   [*At the door*] Come in, Monica. Come in, Emory.

              [*Mrs. Monica Breedlove is a widow of fifty-five or
              so, plump, intelligent, voluble and perhaps over-friendly.
              Her brother, Emory Wages, is a few years younger
              than she, also plump and friendly, but in contrast
              almost taciturn*]

MONICA   Just the effusive neighbors from upstairs, darlings! Have
              to be in on everything. No lives of their own, so they live
              other people's. I speak for my brother as well as myself,
              because he never gets a chance to speak when I'm
              around. There, I've talked enough. Say something, Colo-
              nel.

KENNETH   I guess it will have to be goodbye, because the taxi's here
              and I don't want to rush through traffic.

EMORY   Don't worry about your two pretty girls, Ken. We'll
              keep an eye on them, and if one of them begins to look
              peaked, we'll send up smoke signals.

KENNETH   I'm counting on you, Emory.
              [*He gives Monica his hand*]
              And on Monica.

MONICA   Goodbye.

KENNETH   Well, sweetheart, this is it.
             [*He waves across the room to Rhoda*]
             Goodbye, big eyes!

RHODA   Goodbye, daddy.

CHRISTINE   I promised myself I wouldn't come down, but—

KENNETH   Don't, sweet. It's just another empty month or two.
             We'll get through them somehow.

EMORY   I'm taking these.

             [*He precedes Kenneth out with both bags.* KENNETH
             and CHRISTINE *embrace*]

KENNETH   Goodbye.

             [KENNETH *takes his briefcase and goes out*]

MONICA   Poor boy. He hates to go. And you hate to let him go.

CHRISTINE   I'm—not very self-sufficient.

MONICA   You're in love, both of you, you lucky characters. I
             wish I were. Oh, by the way, nobody has to take Rhoda
             to the bus, because I made some cupcakes for Miss
             Fern, and she's coming by to pick them up.

CHRISTINE   Oh, good.

MONICA   [*To Rhoda*] But before she comes I have two little
             presents for you, my darling.

RHODA   Presents?

MONICA   The first is from Emory. It's a pair of dark glasses with
             rhinestone decorations, and he said to tell you they're
             intended to keep the sun out of those pretty blue eyes.
             [*She produces the glasses, and* RHODA *goes toward her
             with an eager expression which her mother knows as*

Rhoda's "acquisitive look"]
I'll try them on you.
[RHODA *stands obediently while* MONICA *adjusts the glasses*]
Now who is this glamorous Hollywood actress? Can it really be little Rhoda Penmark who lives with her delightful parents on the first floor of my apartment house?

RHODA   [*Looking at her reflection in the glass of a picture*]
               I like them. Where's the case?

MONICA   Here it is. And now for the second prize, which is from me.
               [*She takes from her purse a little gold heart with a chain attached*]
               This was given to me when I was eight years old, and it's a little young for me now, but it's still just right for an eight-year-old. However, it has a garnet set in it, and we'll have to change that for a turquoise, since turquoise is your birthstone. So I'll have it changed and cleaned, and then it's yours.

RHODA   Could I have both stones? The garnet, too?

CHRISTINE   Rhoda! Rhoda! What a—

MONICA   [*Laughing*] But of course you may! How wonderful to meet such a natural little girl! She knows what she wants and asks for it—not like these over-civilized little pets that have to go through analysis before they can choose an ice cream soda!

               [RHODA *goes to her, puts her arms round her waist and hugs her with an intensity which gives Monica great delight*]

RHODA   [*Purring*] Aunt Monica! Dear, sweet Aunt Monica!

               [MONICA *is completely captivated, but* CHRISTINE *looks on with a slightly skeptical and concerned attitude. She knows that Rhoda is not really affectionate, that she is acting*]

MONICA   I know I'm behind the times, but I thought children
            wore coveralls and play-suits to picnics. Now you, my
            love, look like a princess in that red and white dotted
            Swiss. Tell me, aren't you afraid you'll get it dirty?
            Or fall and scuff those new shoes?

CHRISTINE   She won't soil the dress and she won't scuff the shoes.
            Rhoda never gets anything dirty, though how she man-
            ages it, I don't know.

RHODA   I don't like coveralls. They're not—

            [*She hesitates*]

MONICA   You mean coveralls aren't quite ladylike, don't you,
            my darling?
            [*She embraces the tolerant Rhoda again*]
            Oh, you old-fashioned little dear!

RHODA   [*Looking at the locket*] Am I to keep this now?

MONICA   You're to keep it till I find out where I can get the stone
            changed.

RHODA   Then I'll put it in my box.

            [*She goes to her table, opens a drawer and takes out
            a box which once held Swiss chocolates. She opens it
            and places the locket carefully inside.*

            *A voice says "Leroy" as the door swings open. The
            house-man, or* JANITOR, *stands in the doorway*]

LEROY   [*The Janitor*] Guess I'm pretty early, Mrs. Penmark,
            but it's my day for doing the windows on this side.

CHRISTINE   Oh, yes, you can begin in the bedrooms, Leroy.

LEROY   [*To Monica*] Excuse me, ma'am.
            [*To Rhoda*] Mornin'.

            [*He crosses through to the inner hall with pail and
            paraphernalia.* RHODA *skips across the room*]

RHODA   I like garnets, but I like turquoise better.

MONICA   You sound like Fred Astaire, tap-tapping across the
               room. What have you got on your shoes?

RHODA   I run over my heels, and mother had these iron pieces
               put on so they'd last longer.

CHRISTINE   I'm afraid I can't take any credit. It was Rhoda's idea
               entirely.

RHODA   I think they're very nice. They save money.

MONICA   Oh, you penurious little sweetheart! But I'll tell you
               one thing, Rhoda, I think you worry too much when
               you're not the very best at everything. That's one reason
               Emory and I thought you should have some presents
               today. You wanted that penmanship medal very much,
               didn't you?

RHODA   It's the only gold medal Miss Fern gives. And it was
               really mine. Everybody knew I wrote the best hand and
               I should have had it.

               [LEROY *comes through toward the kitchen with his pail*]

LEROY   'Scuse me, just gettin' some water.

               [*He goes to the kitchen*]

RHODA   I just don't see why Claude Daigle got the medal.

CHRISTINE   These things happen to us all the time, Rhoda, and
               when they do we simply accept them. I've told you to
               forget the whole thing.
               [*She puts an arm around Rhoda, trying to soften her.*
               RHODA *pulls away impatiently*]
               I'm sorry. I know you don't like people pawing over
               you.

RHODA   It was mine! The medal was mine!

CHRISTINE   Try to forget it, Rhoda. Put it out of your mind.

RHODA   [*Stamping in anger*] I won't! I won't! I won't!

                 [LEROY *comes out of the kitchen with his pail, passes near Rhoda, and manages to spill a splash of water on her shoes*]

MONICA   Leroy! Have you completely lost your senses? You spilled water on Rhoda's shoes!

LEROY   I'm sorry, ma'am. I guess I was just trying to hurry.

                 [*In turning he spills more water on the floor near Christine*]

MONICA   Leroy!

LEROY   I'm sorry, Mis' Breedlove.

                 [*Kneels*]

MONICA   [*Under her breath*] One, two, three, four, five, six, seven, eight, nine, ten! Leroy, I own this apartment house! I employ you! I've tried to give you the benefit of every doubt! I've thought of you as emotionally immature, torn by irrational rages, a bit on the psychopathic side! But after this demonstration I think my diagnosis was entirely too mild! You're definitely a schizophrenic with paranoid overtones! I've had quite enough of your discourtesy and surliness—and so have the tenants in the building! My brother Emory has wanted to discharge you! I've been on your side, though with misgivings! I shall protect you no longer!

CHRISTINE   He didn't mean it, Monica. It was an accident, I'm sure it was.

RHODA   He meant to do it. I know Leroy well.

MONICA   It was no accident, Christine! It was deliberate—the spiteful act of a neurotic child!

RHODA   He meant to do it. [*To Leroy*] You made up your mind to do it when you went through the room.

CHRISTINE   Rhoda!

RHODA   I was looking at you when you made up your mind to
              wet us.

LEROY   Oh, I never, I never, I'm just clumsy!

              [*He takes out his handkerchief and cleans Rhoda's
              shoes*]

CHRISTINE   [*Not wishing the man to humble himself*] Oh, Leroy,
              please, please!

              [RHODA *draws away*]

MONICA   My patience is at an end, and you may as well know it.
              Go about your work!

LEROY   Yes, ma'am.

              [*He goes out*]

MONICA   He has the mind of an 8-year-old, but he's managed
              to produce a family so I keep him on.
              [*The doorbell rings*]
              It's probably Miss Fern.

CHRISTINE   [*Going to door*] Yes. Come in, Miss Fern. We're nearly
              ready, I think.

MISS FERN   I'm a bit ahead of time, as usual.

              [*She comes in primly. As the head of the most aristo-
              cratic school in the state she has achieved a certain
              savoir faire, though she is in herself a timid and un-
              distinguished little old maid, making the most of the
              remains of once quite remarkable beauty*]

MONICA   Oh, Miss Fern, the old scatterbrain left her two dozen
              cupcakes upstairs. Rhoda, will you help me carry them
              down?

RHODA   Yes, of course I will.

MONICA   They're all packed.

RHODA   [*She curtsies to Miss Fern*] Morning, Miss Fern.

MISS FERN   That's a perfect curtsy, Rhoda.

RHODA   Thank you, Miss Fern.

              [*She goes out the front door with* MONICA]

CHRISTINE   She does such things well?

MISS FERN   She does everything well. As you must know better than I.

CHRISTINE   And, as a person, does she fit in well—at the school?

MISS FERN   Let me think—in what way, Mrs. Penmark?

CHRISTINE   Well, Rhoda has been—I don't quite know how to say it. There's a mature quality about her that's disturbing in a child. My husband and I thought that a school like yours, where you believe in discipline and the old-fashioned virtues, might perhaps teach her to be a bit more of a child.

MISS FERN   Yes—yes, I know what you mean. In some ways, in many ways, Rhoda is the most satisfactory pupil the school has ever had. She's never been absent. She's never been tardy. She's the only child in the history of the school who has made a hundred in deportment each month in every class, and a hundred in self-reliance and conservation on the playground each month for a full school year. If you had dealt with as many children as I have, you'd realize what a remarkable record that is. And she's the neatest little girl I've ever encountered.

CHRISTINE   Kenneth says he doesn't know where she gets her tidiness. Certainly not from him or me.

MISS FERN   She has many good qualities. She's certainly no tattletale.

SALEM COLLEGE LIBRARY
Winston-Salem, North Carolina

CHRISTINE   Oh?

MISS FERN   One of our children broke a window across the street
              and we knew that Rhoda knew who it was. When we
              questioned her about it, and told her it was her duty
              as an honorable citizen to report the offender, she just
              went on eating her apple, shaking her head, denying that
              she knew anything about it—and looking us over with
              that pitying, calculating look she has at certain times.

CHRISTINE   Oh, I know that look so well!

MISS FERN   But that was admirable too, for she was merely being
              loyal to a playmate.

CHRISTINE   Then—do the other children like her? Is she popular?

MISS FERN   The other children? Well, I . . .

              [MISS FERN *hesitates, trying to think of something to
              say, and is saved from having to answer by the re-entry
              of* MONICA *and* RHODA, *carrying two small packed bas-
              kets*]

MONICA   Here we are!

MISS FERN   Then I suppose we should go, for my sisters and the
              others will be waiting. Goodbye, Mrs. Penmark.

CHRISTINE   Goodbye! May it be everything a picnic should be!

MISS FERN   Thank you! Come, Rhoda!

              [*She takes one of the baskets and goes to the door*]

RHODA   Yes, Miss Fern.

              [*She goes to be kissed by her mother*]

MONICA   Calm sea and prosperous voyage!

MISS FERN   Thank you! We'll take care of her!

[RHODA *runs to Monica for a last quick hug*]
No time! We're off!

MONICA   We stole time, didn't we, Rhoda?

MISS FERN   Bless you both!

               [*She goes out with* RHODA]

MONICA   So now the older set's left behind with nothing to do.

CHRISTINE   I could go through the dreary business of trying to make
               my face presentable. It happens every morning.

MONICA   Your face! Think of mine!

CHRISTINE   It always makes me gloomy when Kenneth goes away.
               Anything could happen—before I see him again.
               There's an old saying—we die a little at parting.

MONICA   Oh my dear. We die a little every day if you want to
               brood about it! Why don't we make some kind of party
               of this? You're having Emory and Reginald Tasker
               to lunch—can't I help with that?

CHRISTINE   What does one feed a criminologist?

MONICA   Oh, prussic acid, blue vitriol, ground glass—

CHRISTINE   Hot weather things!

MONICA   Nothing would hurt Reggie. He thrives on buckets of
               blood and sudden death.

CHRISTINE   How many mysteries has he written?

MONICA   A complete set of his works would encircle the Empire
               State building—or me. Come on—I'm a garrulous old
               hag, but I can grind glass. We're not going to let you
               be lonely.

               [*They go into the kitchen together.* LEROY *comes in with
               pail and brush, and opens one of the windows, mutter-
               ing to himself*]

LEROY   That know-it-all, that Monica Breedlove, she don't
          think nobody knows anything but her. I'll show that
          bitch plenty. And that young trough-fed Mrs. Pen-
          mark. She don't get enough of what she needs, and I
          could give it to her. Now Rhoda's smart. That's a
          smart little girl. She's almost as smart as I am. She sees
          through me and I see through her. By damn she's smart.

                         CURTAIN

Act One

SCENE 2

It is 2:30 p.m. the same day. Christine has served lunch in her apartment to Emory Wages and his sister Monica, also to Reginald Tasker, a friend of theirs who writes detective stories and has made himself a minor expert in the history of crime. The luncheon dishes have mostly been removed, and the guests still linger over their iced drinks. The men have taken off their coats. Tasker and Emory are laughing as the curtain goes up.

MONICA   But I did meet him! Nobody ever believes that I met Sigmund Freud—

EMORY   Now, come—they believe you—

MONICA   You mean it's automatic flattery. They know I'm old enough, but they voice doubts to make me feel better— Well, perhaps. Anyway, it wasn't Dr. Freud who analyzed me; it was Dr. Kettlebaum in London.

EMORY   Now we're off.

MONICA   And this was my choice, too. Not that I minimize Freud's professional standing, for I still consider him the great genius of our time—but Dr. Kettlebaum was more—more *sympatico*, if you know what I mean, Reggie.

EMORY   It means *sympatico*, if you know what that means.

MONICA   Freud loathed American women—

CHRISTINE   Oh?

MONICA   Especially those that talked back to him, and I loathed
                his Germanic prejudice against feminine independence,
                which he couldn't conceal.

CHRISTINE   Was Freud prejudiced?

MONICA   Indeed he was. Not consciously, you know. He just
                bristled when I suggested that women had more sense
                than men. Now Dr. Kettlebaum believed in the power
                of the individual soul, and considered sex of only trivial
                interest. His mind was less literal, more mystic, like my
                own.

CHRISTINE   Oh, Monica! Did the analysis do you any good, really?

MONICA   Well, it broke up my marriage. I looked into the very
                bottom of my soul. What a spectacle! When I came
                back I asked Mr. Breedlove for a divorce and he didn't
                oppose it. Then I decided that what I'd always really
                wanted was to make a home for my brother—and so I
                did. I don't think dear Emory appreciates it, but what
                woman—

EMORY   I can stand anything except talk about your analysis—
                and analyzing of your friends—and me. I don't want
                to look at the bottom of my soul.

MONICA   I can understand that perfectly. We're all so sensitive
                about these things. The truth absolutely disgusts us.
                Now I've come to the conclusion that Emory is a "lar-
                vated homosexual"—

CHRISTINE   What?

EMORY   Thank you! What does larvated mean?

MONICA   It means covered as with a masque—concealed.

TASKER   It means something that hasn't come to the surface—
            as yet.

EMORY   You can say that again. If I'm a homosexual, they'll
            have to change the whole concept of what goes on
            among 'em.

TASKER   Where do you get that idea, Monica?

MONICA   Pure association, the best evidence of all. Emory's fifty-
            two years old, and he's never married. I doubt if he's
            ever had a serious love affair.

EMORY   How would you know if they're serious?

MONICA   Please, let's look at things objectively. What are Emory's
            deepest interests in life? They are—
            [She counts them on her fingers]
            fishing, murder mysteries in which housewives are dis-
            membered, canasta, baseball games, and singing in male
            quartets. How does Emory spend Sundays? He spends
            them on a boat with Reggie and other men—fishing.
            And are there ladies present on these occasions? There
            are not.

EMORY   You're damned right there are not!

MONICA   I guess you are all shocked, aren't you? But you
            shouldn't be. Actually, homosexuality is triter than
            incest. Dr. Kettlebaum considered it was all a matter
            of personal preference. I'm perfectly frank about my-
            self. Subconsciously I have an incestuous fixation on
            Emory. It's not normal, but that's the way it is.

EMORY   Thanks a million, little sister. Can't we talk about
            something normal, like murder? Anybody mind if I
            smoke a cigar?

MONICA   What are you trying to prove, Emory?

CHRISTINE   Let's relax away from the table and have our tea over
            here.

MONICA   Yes, we've run thru sex, let's try homicide. Reggie,
              you're the expert.

EMORY   Any change is for the better.

TASKER   All right, I'll oblige. I've been collecting data on Mrs.
              Allison lately. *News Budget* wants an article on her,
              but I can't say she's a very flaming subject. Just an
              unimaginative nurse who decided she was in a position
              to kill folks off for their insurance—and ran through
              quite a list before anybody suspected her.

EMORY   Was this recent?

TASKER   Well, last year and the year before. She'd be going still
              only she was too stupid to vary her poisons, with the
              result that all her victims had similar symptoms—
              nausea, burning throat, intestinal pain and convulsions—
              to say nothing of the conventional life insurance policies
              made out to the old girl with the arsenic.

CHRISTINE   Please, I don't like to hear about such things.

MONICA   You don't?

CHRISTINE   No.

MONICA   Now that's an interesting psychic block. Why would
              Christine dislike hearing about murders?

CHRISTINE   I don't know—I have an aversion to violence of any
              kind. I even hate the revolver Kenneth keeps in the
              house.

MONICA   Oh, do you dislike the revolver more than the poisons?

CHRISTINE   I hate them both.

MONICA   Hmm, perhaps if you'll try saying the first thing that
              comes into your mind we can get at the root anxiety.
              Say it, no matter how silly it seems to you! Tell your
              story, Reggie, and Christine will associate.

EMORY   Oh, nonsense, Monica.

CHRISTINE What do you mean by "associate?"

MONICA   Just speak up—because any idea that comes into your mind will be an associated idea.

CHRISTINE Oh.

TASKER   Well, the end of the story was like this. Toward the middle of May, last year, Mrs. Allison visited her sister-in-law's family. She got there in time for lunch, and her niece Shirley reminded her that she had promised to bring a present for her birthday. Mrs. Allison was so upset about forgetting the present that she went to the neighborhood store and bought candy and soft drinks for the family.

MONICA   [Nudging Christine] Do you think of anything?

CHRISTINE Oh, absolutely nothing.

TASKER   Actually Mrs. Allison had brought her niece a present. It was ten cents' worth of arsenic.

MONICA   But there must be something in your mind—something!

CHRISTINE Well, I was thinking at the moment of how devoted the Fern sisters were to my father, when he was a radio commentator.

MONICA   Hmm—I don't think I understand that—so far. How did you know of this?

CHRISTINE Oh, they spoke of it when I entered Rhoda in their school.

EMORY   Isn't your father Richard Bravo?

CHRISTINE Yes.

EMORY   Yes, I thought so. Well, the whole nation was devoted to him during the last war.

TASKER   Yes, listened to Bravo every evening.

MONICA   Is there any more of the story?

TASKER   Yes. When Mrs. Allison returned from the store she opened a bottle of sarsaparilla for her niece, and then watched the little girl's convulsions for an hour—

MONICA   Now—without thinking at all—what's your second association?
[CHRISTINE *hesitates*]
No editing—no skipping—

CHRISTINE Well, what I was thinking was even sillier. I've always had a feeling that I was an adopted child, and that the Bravos weren't my real parents.

MONICA   Oh, you poor innocent darling! Don't you know that the changeling fantasy is one of the commonest of childhood? I once believed I was a foundling with royal blood—Plantagenet, I think it was. Emory was a Tudor. But have you really always had this—suspicion—that you were adopted?

CHRISTINE Yes, always.

MONICA   But no evidence?

CHRISTINE Only that I dream about it.

MONICA   What kind of dream?

CHRISTINE Oh, Monica, must I tell my dreams too? I'd rather hear the murder story.

MONICA   Well let's hear more story, then hear more from Christine.

EMORY   Why do you always want to dig at people's insides? Monica, you're a ghoul.

MONICA   Of course, who isn't? Furnish the final details, Reggie.

TASKER   Well, Mrs. Allison hurried back to town on an urgent errand. She hadn't paid the current premium on the policy on Shirley's life, and this was the last day of grace.

EMORY   Stupid!

TASKER   Allison was certainly crude. But there have been artists in her line, really gifted operators like Bessie Denker. Bessie never made a mistake, never left a trace, never committed an imperfect crime—

CHRISTINE [*Suddenly interested*] Who was this?

TASKER   The most amazing woman in all the annals of homicide, Bessie Denker. She was beautiful, she was brainy and she was ruthless. She never used the same poison twice. Her own father, for example, died of rabies, contracted supposedly from a mad dog. It just happened that all his money went to Bessie—

CHRISTINE Did you say Bessie Denker?

TASKER   Yes.

CHRISTINE Excuse me. I, I think—I—

EMORY   I guess Christine has had enough of this, Reggie. Couldn't we talk about something else?

TASKER   We certainly could.

MONICA   And we will—though I'm still puzzled—

CHRISTINE No, no—tell us more about Dr. Kettlebaum—

EMORY   If you leave it to Monica, she has three subjects: sex, psychiatry and pills. Sex and psychiatry are synonymous. Better try pills.

MONICA   By pills Emory means the modern pharmaceutical discoveries which have revolutionized medicine since 1935. If you took them, Emory, you'd be a better man.

TASKER   [*Looking at his watch*] I should have looked at this
              before. I've got a lecture date at three-thirty, and I
              won't be much ahead of time if I start now. Will you
              forgive me for filling the air with horror stories, Mrs.
              Penmark?

CHRISTINE   Oh, you must forgive me, Mr. Tasker! I have some
              kind of phobia or mania so that I'm quite unreasonable
              when I hear such things.

TASKER   I'm sick of the bloody stuff myself and only keep on
              with it to make a living—so let's be friends.

              [*He puts out a hand.* CHRISTINE *shakes with him*]

CHRISTINE   Yes, of course.

TASKER   I do have to go. Goodbye, Monica.

MONICA   Goodbye, Bluebeard.

EMORY   Goodbye, Reggie. See you Sunday. I hear the red-fish
              are running.

              [TASKER *goes out*]

TASKER   [*From outside*] Good.

EMORY   I wonder if it wouldn't be about time for the news.
              [*He goes to the radio*]
              Do you mind, Christine?

CHRISTINE   Of course not. I'll just clear these off.

MONICA   I'll lend a hand.

              [*The women carry plates into the kitchen.* EMORY *finds
              the local news broadcast*]

THE RADIO   "Nothing more important has happened for many years
              in the field of foreign affairs."
              [*There is a brief pause, then the voice proceeds on a
              somewhat different note*]

"I interrupt this broadcast to—I have been asked to announce that one of the children on the annual outing of the Fern Grammar School was accidentally drowned in the bay this afternoon. The name of the victim is being withheld until the parents are first notified. More news of the tragic affair is expected momentarily. This is Station WWB—in Tallahassee, bringing you the 3:15 news, brought to you by PICKETS HARDWARE, Best For Your Home Needs."

[MONICA *and* CHRISTINE *hurry into the room, listening.* MONICA *puts her arm around Christine.* EMORY *turns the voice down*]

MONICA   It was not Rhoda. Rhoda is too self-reliant a child. It was some timid, confused youngster, afraid of its own shadow. It certainly wasn't Rhoda.

[EMORY *turns the voice up*]

THE RADIO   "To return to local affairs, I am now authorized to give the name of the victim of the drowning at the Fern School picnic. It was Claude Daigle, the only child of Mr. and Mrs. Dwight Daigle of 126 Willow Street. He appears to have fallen into the water from an abandoned wharf on the Fern property. It is a mystery how the little boy got on the wharf, for all the children had been forbidden to play near or on it, but his body was found off the end of the landing, wedged among the pilings. The guards who brought up the body applied artificial respiration without result. There were bruises on the forehead and hands, but it is assumed these were caused by the body washing against the pilings. And now back to the national news."

[EMORY *turns the radio off*]

CHRISTINE   Poor child—poor little boy!

MONICA   They'll send the children home immediately. They must be on their way now.

EMORY   This will be the end of the picnic.

CHRISTINE   I don't know what to say to her. Rhoda is eight. I re-
                 member I didn't know about death—or it didn't touch
                 me closely—till I was much older. A teacher I adored
                 died. My whole world changed and darkened.

MONICA   We'd better go. This is no time for well-meaning friends
                 to look on from the sidelines.

CHRISTINE   I don't know what to say to her.

EMORY   You'll meet it better alone. Honestly you will.

MONICA   Yes, you will, dear. We'll go. It's between you and
                 Rhoda, dear. Nobody else can help.

CHRISTINE   Yes, I suppose so.

EMORY   Children get these shocks all the time. Life's a grim
                 business.

CHRISTINE   I'm glad you were here. She'll have missed lunch, so
                 I'll make her a sandwich.

MONICA   We'll be upstairs in case you need us.

CHRISTINE   Thank you, Monica. Thank you both.
                 [MONICA *and* EMORY *go out. The clock strikes once—*
                 three-thirty. CHRISTINE *carries some dishes from the*
                 table to the kitchen, leaving the table practically clear.
                 The door opens while she is in the kitchen and RHODA
                 comes in, quiet and unruffled. She sits and removes her
                 shoes. CHRISTINE *re-enters from the kitchen*]
                 Darling!

RHODA   Mother, you know we didn't really have our lunch be-
                 cause Claude Daigle was drowned.

CHRISTINE   I know. It was on the radio.

RHODA   He was drowned, so then they were all rushing and
                 calling and hurrying to see if they could make him alive

again, but they couldn't, so then they said the picnic was over and we had to go home.

CHRISTINE   I'm glad you're home!

RHODA   So could I have a peanut-butter sandwich and milk?

             [CHRISTINE *puts her arm around her*]

CHRISTINE   Did you see him, dear?

RHODA   Yes, of course. Then they put a blanket over him.

CHRISTINE   Did you see him taken from the water?

RHODA   Yes, they laid him out on the lawn and worked and worked. But it didn't help.

CHRISTINE   You must try to get these pictures out of your mind. I don't want you to be frightened or bothered at all. These things happen and we must accept them.

RHODA   I thought it was exciting. Could I have the peanut-butter sandwich?

CHRISTINE   [*Taking away her arm, rising*] Yes, I'm getting it ready for you.
             [*She goes into the kitchen.* RHODA *puts her shoes in the cupboard and takes out skates.* CHRISTINE *enters with a glass of milk and a sandwich as Rhoda sits*]
             Here, dear. Darling, you're controlling yourself very well, but just the same it was an unfortunate thing to see and remember. I understand how you feel, my darling.

RHODA   I don't know what you're talking about. I don't feel any way at all.

             [*She tastes the milk*]

             [CHRISTINE *is puzzled.* RHODA, *feeling that she has displeased her mother somehow, grabs Christine's hand and rubs it against her cheek*]

CHRISTINE   Have you been naughty?

RHODA   Why, no, mother. What will you give me if I give you a basket of kisses?

CHRISTINE   [*Feeling a great rush of affection*] I'll give you a basket of hugs!

RHODA   I want to go out and skate on the asphalt.

CHRISTINE   Then you should, dear.

[CHRISTINE *goes to the kitchen to do the dishes.* RHODA *puts the skates on.* LEROY *opens the door and comes in to empty waste baskets*]

LEROY   [*Under his breath*] How come you go skating and enjoying yourself when your poor little schoolmate is still damp from drowning in the bay? Looks to me like you'd be in the house crying your eyes out; either that or be in church burning a candle in a blue cup.

[RHODA *stares at Leroy but gives no answer. Then with her sandwich in her hand, she gets up and walks on her skates to the door*]

RHODA   'Bye, mother!

CHRISTINE   [*From the kitchen*] Goodbye, Rhoda.

LEROY   Ask me, and I'll say you don't even feel sorry for what happened to that little boy.

RHODA   Why should I feel sorry? It was Claude Daigle got drowned, not me.

[*She goes out.* LEROY *shakes his head*]

CURTAIN

Act One

SCENE 3

It is evening of the same day and Rhoda, ready for bed, is lying on the couch while her mother reads to her. A pillow from her bedroom is under her head, and a half-empty glass sits on the coffee-table beside her.

CHRISTINE   [*Reading*] "Then the knight alit from his steed and sought what way he could find out of this labyrinth, and a path appearing he began to make his way along it and it began at that time to grow dark. The knight had not gone more than a dozen paces before he saw beside the path a beautiful lady who laid out a fair damask cloth under an oak and set thereon cates and dainties and a flagon with two silver cups."

[*She pauses*]

RHODA   Mother?

CHRISTINE   Yes.

RHODA   Why aren't you reading?

CHRISTINE   I was just thinking.

RHODA   What about? The accident?

CHRISTINE   Partly—and about my phone call. The circuits were busy.

27

RHODA   What are cates and dainties?

CHRISTINE   Little cakes, I think.

RHODA   Oh.

CHRISTINE   [*Reading*] . . . "and set thereon cates and dainties and
               a flagon with two silver cups. 'Knight,' she called,
               'knight, come eat and drink with me, for you are hungry
               and thirsty and I am alone.' " Did you take your
               vitamins, dear?

RHODA   [*Sitting up, taking a capsule, sipping from the glass*]
               I took one before. This is the second. I was saving
               them because I like the juice.
               [*She lies back*]
               This is wonderful, to have you read to me out here.

CHRISTINE   You'd better take the third one now.—You'll be too
               sleepy.

RHODA   All right.
               [*She sits up and takes another capsule and the last of
               the drink, then lies back*]
               I'll close my eyes, but I won't be asleep.

CHRISTINE   I know.
               [*She reads*]
               "Then the knight answered her, 'I thank you, fair lady,
               for I am not only hungry and thirsty but I am lost within
               the forest.' Then he let his palfrey graze near-by and he
               feasted with the lady, who gave him loving looks,
               sweeter than the wine from the flagon, though the wine
               was sweet and strong, and in this fashion the time passed
               till the light was gone out of the wood and it was dark."
               [*She pauses*]
               "The knight heard the music of hautbois softly playing
               and he perceived that a fair pavilion stood near-by
               under the oak trees, lighted by a torch at the entrance
               where there were servants going to and fro. And he
               was aware that the pavilion had not been there in the

daylight, but had been created out of darkness—by magic—"

Rhoda? Rhoda?

[*There's no answer.* CHRISTINE *rises, takes the empty glass to the kitchen, returns and bends over Rhoda to pick her up. The phone rings.* CHRISTINE *goes quickly to answer it, so that it won't wake the child. She picks up the receiver*]

Yes, I was calling Washington, D. C. Yes, Bethesda 1293. Mr. Richard Bravo. That's right. Daddy, I'm so glad I found you at home! I've been trying to get you all evening. You said in your letter you might be coming to Tallahassee? Are you well enough to be doing such things? Well that's not really far from here— Couldn't you come to see me? Daddy, couldn't you make it sooner? Could you . . . Well as soon as you can?—No, we're well. It's not that. You met Kenneth at the airport? Tell him I'm writing my first letter to him tonight. I'll send it Air Mail Special in the morning. —Tell him I love him and miss him. And remember I love you and miss you.—No, nothing like that. Daddy, do you remember that recurrent dream I used to have when I was a child?—Now, I'm beginning to have it again and again.—I know what the Freudians say,— but even they tell you dreams can't come out of any past but your own!—Tell me, daddy, is there some terrible thing in my past that I don't know? No—nobody. It's something I dream. Yes, I'll be good. And I will see you? You always help! You always have! I do feel better. Already. Good night, daddy.

[*She hangs up. Rhoda still sleeps.* CHRISTINE *goes to the couch, watches her a moment, then picks her up and carries her to her room.*]

CURTAIN

Act One

SCENE 4

Mid-morning, a few days later, in the same apartment. The living-room is empty; Rhoda can be heard practicing "Au Clair de la Lune" on the piano in the den. Christine is in the kitchen. The doorbell chimes and she answers it. Miss Fern is at the door.

MISS FERN   May I come in, Mrs. Penmark?

CHRISTINE   Yes, of course, Miss Fern. I meant to come and see you. I got your note.

MISS FERN   [*Entering*] We're in such distress, all of us at the school, and we've suffered such a blow, losing one of the children that way, I'm sure you'll excuse us for going over and over things!

CHRISTINE   I think everybody has been puzzled and worried and saddened.

MISS FERN   I don't think I've ever known any happening to puzzle so many people in so many ways. And I can help so few of them. I've just come from seeing Mrs. Daigle. Of course, our first thought was of her. The rest of us are touched only lightly by this tragedy. She will have to live with it the rest of her days.

CHRISTINE   I know.

MISS FERN   I have seen her several times, and each time she has

30

asked me to find out from you if you had any possible clue to where the penmanship medal might be.

CHRISTINE   It was lost?

MISS FERN   Yes, it wasn't found with the body and has completely disappeared.

CHRISTINE   I didn't know of this.

[*At this moment* RHODA *comes out with a book in her hand, dressed immaculately as usual*]

RHODA   [*Curtsying*] Good morning, Miss Fern.

MISS FERN   Good morning, Rhoda.

RHODA   Mother, could I sit under the scuppernong arbor for a while and read my book?

CHRISTINE   Of course, Rhoda.

RHODA   It's shady there, and I can see your window, and you can watch me from the window, and I like to be where you can see me.

CHRISTINE   Is it a new book?

RHODA   Yes. It's *Elsie Dinsmore*. The one I got for a prize at Sunday school.

CHRISTINE   I'll be here.

RHODA   I'll be right there all the time. Goodbye, Miss Fern.

[*Curtsy. She runs out*]

MISS FERN   It did occur to me that—that Rhoda might have told you a detail or two which she hadn't remembered when she talked with me. You see, she was the last to see the little Daigle boy alive—

CHRISTINE   Are you sure of that?

MISS FERN   Yes.

CHRISTINE   I hadn't realized—

MISS FERN   About an hour after we arrived at the estate one of our older pupils came on Rhoda and the Daigle boy at the far end of the grounds. The boy was upset and crying, and Rhoda was standing in front of him, blocking his path. The older girl was among the trees, and neither child saw her. She was just about to intervene when Rhoda shoved the boy and snatched at his medal, but he broke away and ran down the beach in the direction of the old wharf where he was later found. Rhoda followed him, not running, just walking along, taking her time, the older girl said.

CHRISTINE   Has it occurred to you that the older girl might not be telling the truth?

MISS FERN   That isn't at all likely. She was one of the monitors we'd appointed to keep an eye on the younger children. She's fifteen and has been with us since kindergarten days. No, Mrs. Penmark, she was telling precisely what she saw. We know her well.

CHRISTINE   And that was the last time Claude was seen?

MISS FERN   Yes. A little later—it might have been about noon— one of the guards saw Rhoda coming off the wharf. He shouted a warning, but by then she was on the beach again and he decided to forget the matter. The guard didn't identify the girl by name, but she was wearing a red dress, he said, and Rhoda was the only girl who wore a dress that day. At one o'clock the lunch bell rang and Claude was missing when the roll was called. You know the rest, I think.

CHRISTINE   Yes. But this is very serious—that Rhoda was on the wharf—

MISS FERN   Not serious, really, when you've seen as much of how children behave as I have. Children conceal things from adults. Suppose Rhoda did follow the Daigle child onto the wharf—so many things could have happened quite innocently. He may have hidden himself in the old boat-house, and then, when discovered, may have backed away from Rhoda and fallen in the water.

CHRISTINE   Yes, that could have happened.

MISS FERN   Now, Claude, although he looked frail, was an excellent swimmer—and, of course, Rhoda knew that. Once he was in the water she would have expected him to swim ashore. How could she know that the treacherous pilings were at the exact spot where he fell?

CHRISTINE   No.

MISS FERN   Perhaps the thought in Rhoda's mind when he fell in the water was that he'd ruin his new suit and she'd get a scolding for causing it. When he didn't swim ashore at once she may have thought, with the logic of childhood, that he'd hidden under the wharf to frighten her —or to escape her. Later on, when it was too late to do anything, she was afraid to admit what had happened.

CHRISTINE   Then you think she does know something she hasn't told?

MISS FERN   Yes. I think that, like many a frightened soldier, she deserted under fire. This is not a serious charge. Few of us are courageous when tested.

CHRISTINE   She has lied, though.

MISS FERN   Is there any adult who hasn't lied? Smooth the lines from your brow, my dear. You're so much prettier when smiling.

CHRISTINE   I shall question Rhoda.

MISS FERN   I wish you would, though I doubt that you'll learn more than you know.

CHRISTINE   And there's something I want to ask you. There was a
             floral tribute at Claude's funeral sent by the children
             of the Fern School. I suppose the children shared the
             expense—but I haven't been asked to pay my part of it.

MISS FERN   The tribute wasn't nearly so expensive as the papers
             seemed to think. The money has been collected, and
             the flowers paid for.

CHRISTINE   Perhaps you telephoned me, and I was out.

MISS FERN   No, my dear. We thought perhaps you'd want to send
             flowers individually.

CHRISTINE   But why should we have sent flowers individually?
             Rhoda wasn't friendly with the boy, and my husband
             and I had never met the Daigles.

MISS FERN   I don't know, my dear. I really—there are three of us,
             you know, and in the hurry of making decisions—

             [*She pauses*]

CHRISTINE   You make excuses for Rhoda—and then you admit that
             you didn't ask me to help pay for the flowers—and the
             reasons you give for not asking me are obviously
             specious. Does this mean that in your mind, and the
             minds of your sisters, there is some connection between
             the drowning and Rhoda's presence on the wharf?

MISS FERN   I refuse to believe there is any connection.

CHRISTINE   And yet you have acted as if there were.

MISS FERN   Yes, perhaps we have.

CHRISTINE   This is a terrible tragedy for Mrs. Daigle, as you say.
             She has lost her only son. But if there were any shadow
             over Rhoda—from what has happened—I shall have to
             live under it, too—and my husband. As for Rhoda—
             she would not be happy in your school next year.

MISS FERN   No, she would not. And since she would not, it would
             be as well to make up our minds now that she will not
             be there.

CHRISTINE   Then there is a shadow over her—and you have decided
             that she will not be invited to return to the Fern School?

MISS FERN   Yes. We have made that decision.

CHRISTINE   But you can't tell me why?

MISS FERN   I think her behavior in the matter of the medal would
             be sufficient explanation. She has no sense of fair play.
             She's a poor loser. She doesn't play the game.

CHRISTINE   But you're not saying that Rhoda had anything to do
             with Claude's death?

MISS FERN   Of course not! Such a possibility never entered our
             minds!

             [*At this moment the doorbell chimes*]

CHRISTINE   I'd better answer.

MISS FERN   Of course, my dear.

             [CHRISTINE *goes to the door, hesitates a moment, and
             then opens it.* MR. *and* MRS. DAIGLE *come in, he tenta-
             tively, she boldly. She has been drinking*]

CHRISTINE   Yes?

MRS. DAIGLE Thanks. We're Mrs. Daigle and Mr. Daigle. You didn't
             have to let us in, you know. [*To Miss Fern*] You realize
             we followed you. We shouldn't have done it. I'm a little
             drunk. [*To Christine*] I guess you never get a little
             drunk.

CHRISTINE   You're quite welcome, both of you.

MRS. DAIGLE Oh, pay no attention to him. He's all for good-breeding.

He was trying to stop me. Now, you, Mrs. Penmark. You've always had plenty. You're a superior person.

CHRISTINE   No, I'm not.

MRS. DAIGLE Oh, yes. Father was rich. Rich Richard Bravo. I know. Never had to touch dinner. Now I worked in a beauty parlor. Miss Fern used to come there. She looks down on me.

MISS FERN   Please, Mrs. Daigle.

MRS. DAIGLE I was that frumpy blonde. Now I've lost my boy and I'm a lush. Everybody knows it.

MR. DAIGLE   We're worried about Mrs. Daigle. She's under a doctor's care. She's not herself.

MRS. DAIGLE But I know what I'm about just the same. Just the same. May I call you Christine? I'm quite aware that you come from a higher level of society. You prolly made a debut and all that. I always considered Christine such a gentle name. Hortense sounds fat—that's me, Hortense. "My girl Hortense," that's what they used to sing at me, "Hasn't got much sense. Let's write her name on the privy fence." Children can be nasty, don't you think?

MR. DAIGLE   Please, Hortense.

MRS. DAIGLE You're so attractive, Christine. You have such exquisite taste in clothes, but of course you have amples of money to buy 'em with. What I came to see you about, I asked Miss Fern how did Claude happen to lose the medal, and she wouldn't tell me a thing.

MISS FERN   I don't know, Mrs. Daigle. Truly.

MRS. DAIGLE You know more than you're telling. You're a sly one —because of the school. You don't want the school to get a bad name. But you know more than you're telling, Miss Butter-Wouldn't-Melt Fern. There's something

funny about the whole thing. I've said so over and over
to Mr. Daigle. He married quite late, you know. In his
forties. But I wasn't exactly what the fellow calls a
"spring chicken" either. We won't have any more children. No more.

MR. DAIGLE   Please, Hortense. Let me take you home where you can
rest.

MRS. DAIGLE   Rest. Sleep. When you can't sleep at night, you can't
sleep in the daylight. I lie and look at the water where
he went down. There's something funny about the
whole thing, Christine. I heard that your little girl was
the last who saw him alive. Will you ask her about the
last few minutes and tell me what she says? Maybe she
remembers some little thing. I don't care how small it
is! No matter how small! You know something, Miss
Fern dyes her hair! She knows something and she won't
tell me. Oh, my poor little Claude! What did they do to
you?

[CHRISTINE *goes to Mrs. Daigle and puts her arm around
her*]

CHRISTINE   I will ask Rhoda, Hortense. Oh, if I only knew!

MRS. DAIGLE   Somebody took the medal off his shirt, Christine. It
couldn't come off by accident. I pinned it on myself,
and it has a clasp that locks in place. It was no accident. You can wear such simple things, can't you? I
never could wear simple things. I couldn't even buy
'em. When I got 'em home they didn't look simple.—
He was such a lovely, dear little boy. He said I was his
sweetheart. He said he was going to marry me when he
grew up. I used to laugh and say, "You'll forget me long
before then. You'll find a prettier girl, and you'll marry
her." And you know what he said then? He said, "No,
I won't, because there's not a prettier girl in the whole
world than you are." If you don't believe me, ask the
girl who comes in and cleans. She was present at the
time.

MR. DAIGLE   Hortense—Hortense!

MRS. DAIGLE   Why do you put your arms around me? You don't give
a damn about me. You're a superior person and all
that, and I'm—oh, God forgive me! There were those
bruises on his hands, and that peculiar crescent-shaped
mark on his forehead that the undertaker covered up.
He must have bled before he died. That's what the
doctor said. And where's the medal? Who took the
medal? I have a right to know what became of the penmanship medal! If I knew, I'd have a good idea what
happened to him.—I don't know why you took it on
yourself to put your arms around me. I'm as good as
you are. And Claude was better than your girl. He won
the medal, and she didn't.—I'm drunk. It's a pleasure
to stay drunk when your little boy's been killed. Maybe
I'd better lay down.

MR. DAIGLE   We'll go home, and you can lie down there.

MRS. DAIGLE   Why not? Why not go home, and lay down? Goodbye,
all.

MR. DAIGLE   I'm sorry.

MRS. DAIGLE   Oh, who cares what they think? I drank a half bottle
of bonded corn in little sips. I'm drunk as holy hell.

[*The* DAIGLES *go out*]

CHRISTINE   Oh, the poor woman!

MISS FERN   I've tried to think of any little thing I could to tell her.
But nothing helps.

CHRISTINE   Nothing will ever help.

MISS FERN   No.—I'll be getting back. Thank you for bearing with
her, and with me.

CHRISTINE   I'll try again with Rhoda. There's no help for this poor
creature,
[*She indicates the door*]
but I'll try.

MISS FERN   We both have to do what we can. Goodbye, Mrs. Penmark.

CHRISTINE   Goodbye, Miss Fern.
[*She suddenly goes to Miss Fern as she is about to turn
in the doorway, and kisses her, her eyes filling with
tears*]
She will have to live with it till she dies.

MISS FERN   Yes. Till she dies. Thank you.

[*She goes, closing the door.* CHRISTINE *turns and looks
at the apartment, then goes to the window from which
she can see Rhoda. After a moment she waves, and we
know that Rhoda has looked up from her book. The
telephone rings, and* CHRISTINE *answers*]

CHRISTINE   Yes, yes, speaking.—Oh Kenneth, I'm so glad you
called. She's well and I'm well. The little boy who was
drowned? Oh, no, Rhoda's her usual self. She's across
the street where I can look out and see her reading a
book. Do you really, darling?—I hope it won't be too
much longer. Four weeks is a long, long time. Call me
as often as you can, darling. I love you. Then don't be
late. Goodbye, dear.

[*She hangs up and* MONICA *opens the door*]

CHRISTINE   Oh, Monica.

MONICA   Yes, Christine, the fluttery one with the typically inane
conversation, but I do have an errand this time, not
just gab—

CHRISTINE   Come in, please.

MONICA   [*Entering*] It's Rhoda's locket I'm using for an excuse.
I've actually found a place where they'll engrave and
clean it in one day. They didn't agree to this unusual
effort without a little pressure—in fact, I had to
threaten—

CHRISTINE   Not really?

MONICA   Oh, you don't know the old busy-body. She uses pres-
              sure, influence, bribery, blackmail—and I had to pull
              them all on old Mr. Pageson. He said this little job
              would take at least two weeks—

CHRISTINE   I'll get the locket. I know where she keeps it.

MONICA   Good. I told him straight that I'm handling the Com-
              munity Chest again this year, and if he were as busy as
              all that, I'd be happy to revise my estimate of his con-
              tribution upward by a considerable amount.
              [CHRISTINE *has opened Rhoda's table drawer and found
              the locket in the chocolate box. Her fingers feel some-
              thing under the oilcloth lining of the drawer and she
              extracts it also, concealing it from Monica, but turning
              toward her with the locket*]
              Ah, you found it! The darling! She keeps her treasures
              so carefully it's a kind of miserly delight.

CHRISTINE   Shall I wrap it?

MONICA   No, no! I'll just drop it in my purse.
              [*She does so*]
              And now I'll take to the air, dear Christine—only do
              forgive me bursting in and rushing out!

CHRISTINE   No ceremony, please.

MONICA   No ceremony, no; just plain pragmatism! Goodbye,
              darling.

CHRISTINE   Goodbye, Monica.
              [MONICA *goes out.* CHRISTINE *regards the medal in her
              hand with a kind of horror mixed with incredulity.
              After a moment she goes to the window from which
              Rhoda was seen. Evidently Rhoda is not there. She
              turns from the window and sits on the couch, staring at
              the medal. The door opens and* RHODA *comes in quietly*]

RHODA   Did you want me to come in, mother? When you waved?

CHRISTINE   So you had the medal, after all. Claude Daigle's medal.

             [*She puts it on coffee table*]

RHODA   [*Warily*] Where did you find it?

CHRISTINE   How did the penmanship medal happen to be hidden
             under the lining of the drawer of your table? Tell me
             the truth, Rhoda.

             [RHODA *takes off one of her shoes and examines it.
             Then, smiling a little in a fashion she has always found
             charming, she asks—*]

RHODA   When we move into our new house can we have a
             scuppernong arbor, mother? Can we, mother? It's so
             shady, and pretty, and I love sitting in it!

CHRISTINE   Answer my question. And remember I'm not as in-
             nocent about what went on at the picnic as you think.
             Miss Fern has told me a great deal. So please don't
             bother to make up a story for my benefit.
             [RHODA *is silent, her mind working*]
             How did Claude Daigle's medal get in your drawer? It
             certainly didn't get there by itself.
             [RHODA *is silent*]
             I'm waiting for your answer.

RHODA   I don't know how the medal got there, mother. How
             could I?

CHRISTINE   [*Controlling herself*] You know. You know quite well
             how it got there. Did you go on the wharf at any time
             during the picnic? At any time?

RHODA   [*After a pause*] Yes, mother. I—I went there once.

CHRISTINE   Was it before or after you were bothering Claude?

RHODA   I didn't bother Claude, mother. What makes you think
             that?

CHRISTINE   Why did you go on the wharf?

RHODA   It was real early. When we first got there.

CHRISTINE   You knew it was forbidden. Why did you do it?

RHODA   One of the big boys said there were little oysters that grew on the pilings. I wanted to see if they did.

CHRISTINE   One of the guards saw you coming off the wharf. But he says it was just before lunch time.

RHODA   I don't know why he says that. He's wrong, and I told Miss Fern he was wrong. He hollered at me to come off the wharf and I did. I went back to the lawn and that's where I saw Claude. But I wasn't bothering him.

CHRISTINE   What did you say to Claude?

RHODA   I said if I didn't win the medal, I was glad he did.

CHRISTINE   [*Wearily*] Please, please, Rhoda. I know you're an adroit liar. But I must have the truth.

RHODA   But it's all true, mother. Every word.

CHRISTINE   One of the monitors saw you try to snatch the medal off Claude's shirt. Is that true? Every word?

RHODA   Oh, that big girl was Mary Beth Musgrove. She told everybody she saw me. Even Leroy knows she saw me. [*She opens her eyes wide, and smiles as though resolving on complete candor*]
You see, Claude and I were playing a game we made up. He said if I could catch him in ten minutes and touch the medal with my hand—it was like prisoner's base—he'd let me wear the medal for an hour. How can Mary Beth say I took the medal? I didn't.

CHRISTINE   She didn't say you took the medal. She said you grabbed at it. And that Claude ran away down the beach. Did you have the medal even then?

RHODA   No, mommy. Not then.

                   [*She runs to her mother and kisses her ardently. This
                   time* CHRISTINE *is the passive one*]

CHRISTINE   How did you get the medal?

RHODA   Oh, I got it later on.

CHRISTINE   How?

RHODA   Claude went back on his promise and I followed him
                   up the beach. Then he stopped and said I could wear
                   the medal all day if I gave him fifty cents.

CHRISTINE   Is that the truth?

RHODA   [*With slight contempt*] Yes, mother. I gave him fifty
                   cents and he let me wear the medal.

CHRISTINE   Then why didn't you tell this to Miss Fern when she
                   questioned you?

RHODA   Oh, mommy, mommy!
                   [*She whimpers a little*]
                   Miss Fern doesn't like me at all! I was afraid she'd
                   think bad things about me if I told her I had the medal!

CHRISTINE   You knew how much Mrs. Daigle wanted the medal,
                   didn't you?

RHODA   Yes, mother, I guess I did.

CHRISTINE   Why didn't you give it to her?
                   [RHODA *says nothing*]
                   Mrs. Daigle is heart-broken over Claude's death. It's
                   destroyed her. I don't think she'll ever recover from it.
                   [*She disengages herself*]
                   Do you know what I mean?

RHODA   Yes, mother, I guess so, mother.

CHRISTINE   No. You don't know what I mean.

RHODA   It was silly to want to bury the medal pinned on Claude's
             coat. Claude was dead. He wouldn't know whether he
             had the medal pinned on him or not.
             [*She senses her mother's sudden feeling of revulsion,
             and kisses her cheek with hungry kisses*]
             I've got the sweetest mother. I tell everybody I've got the
             sweetest mother in the world!—If she wants a little
             boy that bad, why doesn't she take one out of the
             Orphans' Home?

CHRISTINE   Don't touch me! Don't talk to me! We have nothing to
             say to each other!

RHODA   Well, okay. Okay, mother.

             [*She turns away and starts to the den*]

CHRISTINE   Rhoda! When we lived in Baltimore, there was an old
             lady, Mrs. Clara Post, who liked you very much.

RHODA   Yes.

CHRISTINE   You used to go up to see her every afternoon. She was
             very old, and liked to show you all her treasures. The
             one you admired most was a crystal ball, in which opals
             floated. The old lady promised this treasure to you
             when she died. One afternoon when the daughter was
             shopping at the super-market, and you were alone with
             Mrs. Post, the old lady somehow managed to fall down
             the spiral backstairs and break her neck. You said she
             heard a kitten mewing outside and went to see about it
             and somehow missed her footing and fell five flights to
             the courtyard below.

RHODA   Yes, it's true.

CHRISTINE   Then you asked the daughter for the crystal ball. She
             gave it to you, and it's still hanging at the head of your
             bed.

RHODA   Yes, mother.

CHRISTINE   Did you have anything to do, anything at all, no matter how little it was, with Claude getting drowned?

RHODA   What makes you ask that, mother?

CHRISTINE   Come here, Rhoda. Look me in the eyes and tell me. I must know.

RHODA   No, mother. I didn't.

CHRISTINE   You're not going back to the Fern School next year. They don't want you any more.

RHODA   Okay. Okay.

CHRISTINE   [*Crosses to telephone*] I'll call Miss Fern and ask her to come over.

RHODA   She'll think I lied to her.

CHRISTINE   You did lie to her!

RHODA   But not to you, mother! Not to you!

             [CHRISTINE *rises and goes to the telephone.* RHODA *watches her with apprehension.* CHRISTINE *dials a number*]

CHRISTINE   The Fern School? Is Miss Claudia Fern there?—No. No message.
             [*She hangs up*]
             She's not home yet.

RHODA   What would you tell her, mother?

CHRISTINE   No! It can't be true! It can't be true!

             [*She turns and looks at Rhoda; then embraces her*]

                         CURTAIN

Act Two

SCENE 1

The same apartment, late afternoon, the next day. Rhoda is seated at her little table putting a jig-saw puzzle together. She works with intense concentration, trying, rejecting, considering sizes and angles. Christine comes out of the inner hall after Rhoda calls.

MONICA   Anybody here?

RHODA   Hello, Aunt Monica!

MONICA   Hi, honey.

RHODA   Mother!

MONICA   Oh, Christine! You said I might have Rhoda for a while. And there's a package for you.

CHRISTINE   Thank you, Monica. You're always the bringer of gifts.

    [*She takes a rather bulky carton from Monica*]

MONICA   This is from somebody else. It was in the package room.

CHRISTINE   Oh—for Rhoda, from daddy—

RHODA   [*Up at once*] For me?

CHRISTINE   Oh, not yet. "In anticipation of her ninth birthday."

RHODA   What does anticipation mean?

MONICA   Looking forward to it.

CHRISTINE   "Not to be opened till—"

RHODA   Oh. It's a long time to wait. But I will.

MONICA   Isn't she the perfect old-fashioned girl? She'll wait!

CHRISTINE   No—there's more in daddy's writing— "Open when you
            get it—there'll be a real one later."

RHODA   But then he wants me to open it now!

CHRISTINE   Yes. All it needs is to be slit down this side with the
            scissors.

RHODA   There's excelsior—I can see it.

CHRISTINE   It should be opened in the kitchen, Rhoda.

RHODA   Okay.

            [*She takes the package to the kitchen*]

MONICA   [*Watching Rhoda, waiting till she's out of earshot*] I wish
            she were mine! Every time I look at her I wish I had
            just such a little girl.

CHRISTINE   She's not wanted in the Fern School next year.

MONICA   Why?

CHRISTINE   She doesn't fit in, doesn't play the game, she's a poor
            sport.

MONICA   Honestly, the longer I live, the more I see, the less I'm
            able to understand the tight little minds of people like
            the Fern girls! The truth of the matter is, Rhoda is much
            too charming, too clever, too unusual for them! She

makes those others look stupid and stodgy by compari-
son!
[*She lights a cigarette*]
Have one?

CHRISTINE   I seem to have quit.

MONICA   Seem to have! Good God, if I were to quit you'd hear
the repercussions in New Orleans! I string along with
St. Paul—it's better to smoke than to burn.—Could
Rhoda stay up and have dinner with me tonight?

CHRISTINE   Yes, she could. I've asked Reginald Tasker over for
cocktails and to talk to me about some writing I want
to try.

MONICA   Fine; there's no reason why Rhoda should hear about his
strychnines and belladonnas.
[RHODA *comes to the kitchen door with a large paste-
board box in her hands*]
Rhoda, you're to have dinner with me tonight.

RHODA   I am? May I bring my new puzzle?

MONICA   You surely may.

CHRISTINE   Is that what it was?

RHODA   I think it must be the best jig-saw puzzle in the whole
world.

[*There is a tap at the door and as* LEROY *speaks it
swings open*]

LEROY   [*Outside*] Leroy.

[LEROY *enters with a garbage pail*]

RHODA   Oh, Leroy, there was a lot of excelsior.

MONICA   He'll take care of it.

LEROY   Yes, surely, ma'am.

CHRISTINE   Don't bother to sweep the kitchen. I'll do it.

             [LEROY *carries the garbage pail into the kitchen*]

RHODA   It's a map of Asia with all the animals.

MONICA   I have an aversion to cobras, but it's Freudian.

LEROY   [*Emerging from the kitchen*] There's a lot of this stuff
             scattered around, Mis' Penmark.

MONICA   Let him sweep it, dear. I shall run up and look at the
             simmering meat sauce.

RHODA   Oh, is it spaghetti?

MONICA   It is. Approve?

RHODA   My favorite!

MONICA   Come up any time. It must be nearly ready.

             [*She goes out.* LEROY *begins to sweep in the kitchen.*
             RHODA *puts her new puzzle on the table and examines
             it*]

MESSENGER   [*In the hall outside*] Mrs. Penmark?

MONICA   Yes. This is her door.
             [MONICA *looks in*]
             Western Union for you, dear.

CHRISTINE   Thank you.
             [MONICA *disappears, leaving a messenger in her place
             in the doorway. He hands Christine a yellow envelope.
             She takes the envelope and the messenger goes, closing
             the door.* CHRISTINE *opens the envelope, and reads the
             message with pleasure*]
             Ah!

RHODA   Is it daddy?

CHRISTINE   Not your daddy this time; mine. He's coming here.

RHODA   Grandfather?

CHRISTINE   Yes. He'll be here tonight.—He can sleep—I think
               Monica has an extra room—I must run up and ask her!
               Be right back.

               [*She goes out.* LEROY *comes from the kitchen again
               with the box of excelsior*]

LEROY   [*Quietly*] There she sits at her little table, doing her
               puzzle and looking cute and innocent. Looking like she
               wouldn't melt butter, she's that cool. She can fool some
               people with that innocent look she can put on and put
               off when she wants to, but not me. Not even part way,
               she can't fool me.
               [RHODA *looks at Leroy as though he bored her, then
               turns back to the puzzle*]
               She don't want to talk to nobody smart. She likes to
               talk to people she can fool, like her mama and Mrs.
               Breedlove and Mr. Emory.

RHODA   Go empty the excelsior. You talk silly all the time. I
               know what you do with the excelsior. You made a bed
               of excelsior in the garage behind that old couch, and
               you sleep there where nobody can see you.

LEROY   I been way behind the times here-to-fore, but now I got
               your number, miss. I been hearing things about you that
               ain't nice. I been hearing you beat up that poor little
               Claude in the woods, and it took all three the Fern
               sisters to pull you off him. I heard you run him off the
               wharf, he was so scared.

RHODA   [*Picking up a piece*] If you tell lies like that you won't
               go to heaven when you die.

LEROY   I heard plenty. I listen to people talk. Not like you who's
               gabbling all the time and won't let anybody get a word

in edgewise. That's why I know what people are saying
and you don't.

RHODA   People tell lies all the time. I think you tell them more
than anybody else.

LEROY   I know what you done to that boy when you got him out
on the wharf. You better listen to me if you want to
keep out of bad trouble.

RHODA   What did I do, if you know so much?

LEROY   You picked up a stick and hit him with it. You hit him
because he wouldn't give you that medal like you told
him to. I thought I'd seen some mean little girls in my
time, but you're the meanest. You want to know how
I know how mean you are? Because I'm mean. I'm
smart and I'm mean. And you're smart and you're
mean, and I never get caught and you never get caught.

RHODA   I know what you think. I know everything you think.
Nobody believes anything you say.

LEROY   You want to know what you did after you hit that boy?
You jerked the medal off his shirt. Then you rolled that
sweet little boy off the wharf, among them pilings.

RHODA   You don't know anything. None of what you said is
true.

LEROY   You know I'm telling the God's truth. You know I got it
figured out.

RHODA   You figured out something that never happened. And
so it's all lies. Take your excelsior down to the garage
and put it where you can sleep on it when you're supposed to be working.

LEROY   You ain't no dope—that I must say—and that's why
you didn't leave that stick where nobody could find it.
Oh, no, you got better sense than that. You took that
bloody stick and washed it off good, and then you threw
it in the woods where nobody could see it.

RHODA   I think you're a very silly man.

LEROY   It was you was silly, because you thought you could
             wash off blood—and you can't.

RHODA   [*After a pause, putting down a piece*] Why can't you
             wash off blood?

LEROY   Because you can't, and the police know it. You can
             wash and wash, but there's always some left. Every-
             body knows that. I'm going to call the police and tell
             them to start looking for that stick in the woods. They
             got what they call "stick bloodhounds" to help them
             look—and them stick bloodhounds can find any stick
             there is that's got blood on it. And when they bring in
             that stick you washed so clean the police'll sprinkle that
             special blood powder on it, and that little boy's blood
             will show up on the stick. It'll show up a pretty blue
             color like a robin's egg.

RHODA   You're scared about the police yourself!

LEROY   Shhh!

RHODA   What you say about me, it's all about you! They'll get
             you with that powder!

             [LEROY *hears Mrs. Penmark coming*]

LEROY   As far as I'm concerned I wish there was more excelsior.
             I could use it.

CHRISTINE   [*Coming in*] What were you saying to Rhoda?

LEROY   Why, Mrs. Penmark, we was just talking. She said it
             was a big box of excelsior.

CHRISTINE   [*Seeing the anger on Rhoda's face, the smirk of triumph
             on Leroy's*] Just the same you're not to speak to her
             again. If you do I'll report you! Is that entirely clear?

RHODA   I started it, mama. I told him it was a puzzle all about
             Asia, and I hardly know where anything is in Asia.

CHRISTINE   Very well—but don't speak to her!

LEROY   Yes, ma'am.

             [*He goes*]

CHRISTINE   [*Turning on the lights*] You're really working in the
             dark here. I think you strain your eyes over these
             things.

             [CHRISTINE *wheels a small bar out of the kitchen, set
             up to serve drinks*]

RHODA   Mother, is it true that when blood has been washed off
             anything a policeman can still find it was there if he
             puts powder on the place? Will the place really turn
             blue?

CHRISTINE   Who's been talking to you about such things? Leroy?

RHODA   No, mommy, it wasn't he. It was some man went by the
             gate in the park.

CHRISTINE   I don't know how they test for blood. But I could ask
             Reginald Tasker. Or Miss Fern; she might know.

RHODA   No—don't ask her! Mommy, mommy, mommy!
             [*She breaks down and cries, deliberately*]
             Nobody helps me! Nobody believes me! I'm your little
             girl, and I'm all alone!

CHRISTINE   It's not a very good act, Rhoda. You may improve it
             enough to convince someone who doesn't know you,
             but at present it's easy to see through.

RHODA   [*Wiping away tears with the back of her hand*] Maybe
             I'd better go up to Monica's and have dinner.

CHRISTINE   Yes. She said any time.
             [*The doorbell rings*]
             And my company is here.
             [*She opens the door*]
             Good evening, Mr. Tasker.

TASKER   Good evening.

CHRISTINE   This is my daughter, Rhoda.

TASKER   [*Entering*] Thanks. Hello, Rhoda.
              [*He puts out his hand. She takes it and gives him her*
              best smile]
              Well, isn't she a little sweetheart!

RHODA   [*Making her curtsy*] Thank you.

TASKER   That's the kind of thing makes an old bachelor wish he
              were married.

RHODA   You like little girls to curtsy?

TASKER   It's the best thing left out of the Middle Ages!

RHODA   I'm having dinner upstairs.

TASKER   The loss is ours, all ours.

CHRISTINE   You may go now, Rhoda.

RHODA   Yes, mommy.

              [*She throws Christine a kiss and runs out*]

TASKER   That's a little ray of sunshine, that one. Isn't she?

CHRISTINE   I've seen her stormy.

TASKER   No doubt. But she's going to make some man very
              happy. Just that smile.

CHRISTINE   Since I called you I've had a wire from my father, and
              he'll be here tonight. It's a year since I've seen him.

TASKER   Bravo's coming?

CHRISTINE   Yes.

TASKER   Now there's a man I always wanted to meet.

CHRISTINE   He may be here before long. He said perhaps for dinner.

TASKER   Good. By the way, if you're thinking of writing mystery stories Bravo was quite an authority on crime and criminals early in his career.

CHRISTINE   Yes, I know he was.

TASKER   He could probably help you more than I could. Before he began covering wars he covered practically all the horror cases, from Leopold and Loeb on.

CHRISTINE   What will it be?

TASKER   Gin and tonic?

CHRISTINE   Good. I'll have it too.—You see, what I wanted to ask was a psychological question and I doubt that it was asked or answered—if it has been—till recently.

             [*She pauses, pouring into the jigger, getting out the ice*]

TASKER   I may not know all the answers.

CHRISTINE   Well, perhaps nobody does. But the story I was thinking of writing made me wonder—tell me, do children ever commit murders? Or is crime something that's learned gradually, and grows as the criminal grows up, so that only adults do really dreadful things?

TASKER   Well, I have thought about that, and so have several authorities I've consulted lately. Yes, children have often committed murders, and quite clever ones too. Some murderers, particularly the distinguished ones who are going to make great names for themselves, start amazingly early.

CHRISTINE   In childhood?

TASKER   Oh, yes. Just like mathematicians and musicians. Poets develop later. There's never been anything worth while in poetry written before eighteen or twenty. But Mozart showed his genius at six, Pascal was a master mathematician at twelve, and some of the great criminals were top-flight operators before they got out of short pants and pinafores.

CHRISTINE   They grew up in the slums, or among criminals, and learned from their environment?
[*The doorbell chimes*]
Oh—I wonder if that could be father!

TASKER   If it is I would like to stay and see him a moment—

CHRISTINE   Oh, that's understood!
[*She opens the door*]
Daddy!

[BRAVO *comes into the doorway, a man of fifty-five or sixty, handsome once, but somewhat stern and weary*]

BRAVO   Hello, darling. I'm early.

[CHRISTINE *goes into his arms and they kiss, then stand looking at each other. He sets down a small bag*]

CHRISTINE   You're here! You're actually here!

BRAVO   I guess I'm something of a truant, sweetheart, but you said you wanted to see me, and I wanted to see you, so—

CHRISTINE   I'm so glad! This is Reginald Tasker, father.

BRAVO   [*Giving his hand to Tasker*] Ah, one of my favorites!

TASKER   Puts you to sleep regularly?

BRAVO   Sometimes keeps me awake. You've done some impressive research for the Classic Crime Club.

TASKER   Now I've always thought the best papers they ever printed were by Richard Bravo.

BRAVO   That old dodo! No, no, he's written himself out, and talked himself out and now he's drifting round the country, working for a second-rate news service.

TASKER   You're really looking into this off-side oil?

BRAVO   That's what they've got me doing. But I took off and left them, for the moment anyway. I wanted to see my long-lost daughter.

[*He puts his arm around Christine*]

TASKER   I've sometimes wanted to ask you if you've ever considered coming back into the criminology racket. There's been nobody like you since you left.

BRAVO   Well, all compliments aside, my latest books didn't sell as well as the first one—and the war came along. Now I write filler.

TASKER   You've written some things that won't be forgotten.

BRAVO   Let's hope.

TASKER   And now your daughter is going to try her hand.

BRAVO   At writing? She can't even spell.

CHRISTINE   I do get lonely here with Kenneth away, and I thought I'd try to work out a murder mystery, in the evenings.

BRAVO   [*To Tasker*] And you're encouraging this competition?

TASKER   Well, I was rather stumped by her last question. She was asking whether criminal children are always the product of environment.

BRAVO   Nothing difficult about that, little one. They are.

TASKER   Now, I'd have said the same, a few years ago—

BRAVO   Look, can't I have some of this wicked mixture you're lapping up?

CHRISTINE   Of course, daddy—I'm sorry. Do you really think they're always the product of environment?

BRAVO   Always.

TASKER   I couldn't prove you're wrong, of course. But some doctor friends of mine assure me that we've all been putting too much emphasis on environment and too little on heredity lately. They say there's a type of criminal born with no capacity for remorse or guilt— born with the kind of brain that may have been normal among humans fifty thousand years ago—

BRAVO   Do you believe this?

TASKER   Well, yes, I guess I do.

BRAVO   Well, I don't.

TASKER   I've been convinced that there are people—only a few, and certainly very unfortunate—who are incapable from the beginning of acquiring a conscience, or a moral character. Not even able to love, except physically. No feeling for right or wrong.

BRAVO   I've heard such assertions, but never found any evidence behind them. If you encounter a human without compassion or pity or morals, he grew up where these things weren't encouraged. That's final and absolute. This stuff you're talking is tommyrot.

             [He sips his drink]

CHRISTINE   Do your doctor friends have any evidence?

TASKER   They can't prove it, but they think there are such people. They say there are children born into the best families, with every advantage of education and discipline—that never acquire any moral scruples. It's as if they were born blind—you couldn't expect to teach them to see.

CHRISTINE   And do they look—like brutes?

BRAVO   Are you sold on this?

CHRISTINE I want to find out.

TASKER   Sometimes they do. But often they present a more convincing picture of virtue than normal folks. A wax rosebud or a plastic peach can look more perfect than the real thing. They imitate humanity beautifully.

CHRISTINE But that's—horrible.

TASKER   Some of them seem to have done some pretty horrible things and kept on looking innocent and sweet.

BRAVO   I'd like to examine the evidence. Not much sense discussing it till we do.

TASKER   Well, this clinic I frequent came long ago to the conclusion that there are bad seeds—just plain bad from the beginning, and nothing can change them.

CHRISTINE And this favorite murderess of yours—the one you were speaking of the other day—is she an instance?

TASKER   Bessie Denker—was she a bad seed? Well, she may have been, because the deaths started so early in her vicinity. Bessie earned her sobriquet of "The Destroying Angel" in early childhood.

CHRISTINE Then she began young?

TASKER   Yes. The name wasn't applied to her till much later, when the whole story of her career came out, but Bessie was lethal and accurate from the beginning. One of her most famous murders involved the use of the deadly amanita, a mushroom known as "the destroying angel," and some clever reporter transferred the term to her. —In fact, it was a colleague of Mr. Bravo's, unless I've misread something—

BRAVO   It may have been—I don't know.

CHRISTINE How did she end?

TASKER   Well, Mr. Bravo knows more about it than I do—

BRAVO   I've forgotten the whole thing. Put it out of my mind.
            I'm in oil now.

CHRISTINE   Tell me—how did she end?

BRAVO   You don't want to probe into this mess, sweetheart—

CHRISTINE   Yes, I do.

BRAVO   Can't we change the subject?

CHRISTINE   No, darling, I want to know. What was the rest of the
            story, Mr. Tasker?

TASKER   There's the mystery. By the time the authorities got
            really roused about her she disappeared from the Middle
            West—just seemed to vanish. She had quite a fortune
            by that time. The fellow that seems to know most about
            her maintains that she went to Australia. A similar
            beauty emerged in Melbourne; her name was Beulah
            Demerest, so if it was the same person she didn't have
            to change the initials on her linen or silver.

CHRISTINE   How could she—kill so many—and leave no trace?

TASKER   [*To Bravo*] You wrote a famous essay listing all her
            methods—you must know it better than I do—

BRAVO   Not at all. I've dropped all that—haven't read the
            recent literature.

CHRISTINE   Did she ever use violence?

TASKER   Forgive me, sir, I'll make it short. She made a specialty
            of poisons—studied not only drugs and toxins but the
            lives of those she wished to kill. It's practically impos-
            sible to prove murder when the victim dies of rattlesnake
            venom in Western Colorado. Too many diamond-backs
            about. And tetanus can be picked up in any barnyard.
            She made use of such things.—It all came to a sudden

end—she was indicted again and took off for parts unknown—leaving no—but wasn't there a child, a little girl?

BRAVO   Never heard of one. That must be a recent addition to the myth.

CHRISTINE   I wanted to ask one more question. Was she ever found out here?

TASKER   Not in this country. Three juries looked at that lovely dewy face and heard that melting cultured voice and said, "She couldn't have done it."

CHRISTINE   She wasn't convicted?

TASKER   "Not guilty." Three times.

CHRISTINE   You think she was one of these poor deformed children, born without pity?

TASKER   Personally, I guess I do.

CHRISTINE   Did she have an enchanting smile?

TASKER   Dazzling, by all accounts.

CHRISTINE   She was doomed?

TASKER   Absolutely. Doomed to commit murder after murder till somehow or other she was found out.

CHRISTINE   She'd have been better off if she'd died young.

TASKER   And society would. And yet sometimes I wonder whether these malignant brutes may not be the mutation that survives on this planet in this age. This age of technology and murder-for-empire. Maybe the softies will have to go, and the snake-hearted will inherit the earth.

BRAVO   I'm betting on the democracies.

TASKER   And so am I. But we're living in an age of murder. In all history there have never been so many people murdered as in our century. Add up all the murders from the beginning of history to 1900, and then add the murders after 1900, and our century wins. All alone. —And on that merry note I think I should take my leave, for I meant not to bother you and I've been lecturing.

BRAVO   You've got a highly questionable theory there—about heredity.

TASKER   I'd like to go into that with you when there's more time.

BRAVO   Let's do that next time I'm in town.

TASKER   Right. And now I'll say good evening, Mrs. Penmark— I'm afraid the pleasure's been all mine.

CHRISTINE Not at all. I'll call you early in the week.

TASKER   I'm always about. [*To Bravo*] Good night, sir.

BRAVO   Good night, Mr. Tasker.

CHRISTINE Good night.

           [TASKER *goes out*]

BRAVO   Are you really planning to write something?

CHRISTINE I was just asking questions. You saw Kenneth in Washington?

BRAVO   Yes. He's looking well. As well as possible when a fellow's hot, sticky, tired, and, most of all, lonesome.

CHRISTINE We'd counted on going somewhere this summer. Then there was a sudden change of orders.

BRAVO   Am I looking too close, or is there something heavy on your mind?

CHRISTINE   Does something show in my face?

BRAVO   Everything shows in your face. It always did.

CHRISTINE   I'm not sure I'm worried about anything—now that
             you're here. I always felt so safe and comfortable when
             you were in the room. And you have the same effect
             now.

BRAVO   To tell you the truth you did a magic for me. I'd always
             wanted a little girl and you were everything lovely a
             little girl could be for her old dad. But, Christine, what
             did you want to ask me—that night you phoned?

CHRISTINE   Let me think a minute.—Would you have another
             drink?

BRAVO   Yes, I guess I will.
             [*He looks at the bar*]
             Let me fix something. Will you have more gin and tonic?

             [*He goes to the bar*]

CHRISTINE   No, thank you.

BRAVO   Speak up, darling. It's between us, whatever it is.

CHRISTINE   My landlady here is—is a sort of amateur psychiatrist—
             a devotee of Freud, constantly analyzing.

BRAVO   I know the sort.

CHRISTINE   Her name is Breedlove. You'll meet her, because she's
             offered a wonderful room for you to stay in while you're
             here. Rhoda's having dinner with her tonight.

BRAVO   You were going to come out with something.

CHRISTINE   Yes. Well, what I was going to ask reminded me of her.
             I confessed to her the other day that I had always wor-
             ried about being an adopted child—had always been
             afraid that mommy wasn't really my mother and the
             daddy I love so much wasn't really my daddy.

BRAVO   What did she say?

CHRISTINE   She said it was one of the commonest fantasies of child-
             hood. Everybody has it. She had it herself.

BRAVO   It certainly is common.

CHRISTINE   But that doesn't help me. I still feel, just as strongly as
             ever, that old fear that you're not really mine.

BRAVO   Has something made you think of this lately?

CHRISTINE   Yes.

BRAVO   What is it?

CHRISTINE   My little girl, Rhoda.

BRAVO   What about her?

CHRISTINE   She terrifies me. I'm afraid for her. I'm afraid of what
             she may have inherited from me.

BRAVO   What could she have inherited?

CHRISTINE   Father—daddy—whose child am I?

BRAVO   Mine.

CHRISTINE   Daddy, dear, don't lie to me. It's gone beyond where
             that will help. I've told you about a dream I have—and
             I'm not sure it's all a dream. Whose child am I? Are
             you my father?
             [BRAVO *is silent*]
             This is a strange question to greet you with after being
             so long away from you—but I—I have to ask it. And
             for Rhoda's sake—and mine—you must tell me.

BRAVO   What has Rhoda done?

CHRISTINE   I don't know. But I'm afraid.

BRAVO   It cannot be inherited. It cannot.

         [*He draws a deep breath, then takes a step and staggers slightly, putting out a hand for support*]

CHRISTINE   Father, you're not well!

         [*She goes to him. He sinks into a chair*]

BRAVO   I'm all right, just get me a glass of water.
         [*She gets a glass from the kitchen*]
         Perfectly well. A trace of fibrillation once in a while, quite normal at my age. Thank you. And with fibrillation there's a slight dizziness, also normal. I'm all right now.

CHRISTINE   I won't ask any more questions. I'm sorry.

BRAVO   I think that's better. Let's just close the book.

CHRISTINE   [*After a pause*] Only I have the answer now.

BRAVO   The answer?

CHRISTINE   Yes.

BRAVO   I've been a very fortunate man, Christine. I could tell you a long history of jobs that came in the nick of time, of lost money found, of friends who showed up to pay old debts just when I had to have the money. At every main turning-point in my life some good fairy has seemed to intervene to flip things my way. And the biggest piece of luck I ever had—the luck that saved my reason and kept me going—was a little girl named Christine. You were the only child I ever had. My life was futile and barren before you came, but you were magic for me, as I said, and you made life bearable. I kept on—because of you.

CHRISTINE   You don't have to say any more.

BRAVO   I don't, do I?

CHRISTINE   You found me somewhere.

BRAVO   Yes. In a very strange place—in a strange way.

CHRISTINE   I know the place.

BRAVO   I don't think you could. You were less than two years old.

CHRISTINE   I either remember it or I dreamed it.

BRAVO   What kind of dream?

CHRISTINE   I dream of a bedroom in a farmhouse in a countryside where there are orchards. I sleep in the room with my brother, who is older than I—and my—is it my mother? —comes to take care of him. She is a graceful, lovely woman, like an angel. I suppose my brother must have died, for afterward I'm alone in the room. One night I awake feeling terrified and for some reason I can't stay in that house. It's moonlight and I somehow get out the window, drop to the grass below and hide myself in the tall weeds beyond the first orchard. I don't recall much more except that toward morning I'm thirsty and keep eating the yellow pippins that fall from the tree— and when the first light comes up on the clouds I can hear my mother calling my name. I hide in the weeds and don't answer. Is this a dream? Is it only a dream?

BRAVO   What name did she call?

CHRISTINE   It isn't Christine. It—is it—could it be Ingold?

BRAVO   You remember that name?

CHRISTINE   Yes, it comes back to me. "Ingold! Ingold Denker," she was calling. Denker? You've concealed something from me all these years, haven't you, daddy? I came out of that terrible household! You found me there!

BRAVO   The neighbors found you after your mother vanished. Where she went I never knew, nor did they, but she had quite a fortune by that time, and something had panicked her—so she quickly got away, leaving one child, an astonishingly sweet and beautiful little thing with the most enchanting smile I've ever seen. I was covering the case for a Chicago paper, and I wired my wife to join me. We couldn't resist you.

CHRISTINE   Oh, daddy, daddy! Oh, God help me! Why didn't you leave me there? Why didn't I die in the orchard and end the agony then?

BRAVO   It was the neighbors found you and saved you. Would you rather have stayed with them?

CHRISTINE   Oh, no, you know I wouldn't. You've been a wonderful father! But—that place—and that evil woman—my mother—!

BRAVO   There are places and events in every man's life he'd rather not remember. Don't let it hurt you now. It's past and doesn't touch you.

CHRISTINE   I wish I had died then! I wish it! I wish it!

BRAVO   It hasn't mattered where you came from! You've been sound and sweet and loving! You've given me more than I ever gave or could ever repay! If you'd been my own I couldn't have hoped for more! You knew nothing but love and kindness and you've given love and kindness and sweetness all your life! Kenneth loves you, and you've made him happy. And Rhoda's a perfect, sweet, sound little girl!

CHRISTINE   Is she, father? Is she?

BRAVO   What has she done?

CHRISTINE   She's—it's as if she were born blind!

BRAVO   It cannot happen! It does not happen!

[*The doorbell chimes and* MONICA *comes in*]

MONICA   Excuse me, please, but Rhoda has eaten her dinner, tired of her puzzle and now she wants a book.

CHRISTINE   We haven't even started yet.

MONICA   And I haven't met Mr. Bravo.
             [*She puts out her hand*]
             I'm Mrs. Breedlove. The oversized analyst who's going to put you up, and promises not to annoy you.

BRAVO   You know what newspaper men are like—crusty, bitter, irascible. If you can put up with me you're a saint.

             [RHODA *enters*]

RHODA   Granddaddy!

BRAVO   Rhoda!

             [*He picks her up and puts her down*]

MONICA   Isn't she perfection?

RHODA   Next to daddy, you lift me up best! Why do you look at me?

BRAVO   I want to see your face.

MONICA   You know, Mr. Bravo, these Penmarks are the most enchanting neighbors I've ever had. Now I'll want Rhoda for dinner every night. Tell me, didn't you write the FINGERPRINT SERIES?

BRAVO   I'm afraid I was very guilty of that about twenty years ago.

MONICA   I read the first volume to pieces, and wept over it till the parts I loved most were illegible—and then bought another!

BRAVO   I've finally met my public.

MONICA   I don't disappoint you? Anyway I'm large.

BRAVO   I like the way you read books to pieces. It's good for royalties.

CHRISTINE   It's time to get dinner for us.

BRAVO   Maybe I should find my room and get ready for the evening.

MONICA   I'll take you up if you'd like to go now.

BRAVO   If you'll be so kind.

MONICA   It's the floor above. Be back, Christine.

               [BRAVO *picks up his small bag and goes out with* MONICA. CHRISTINE *goes into the kitchen to get dinner.* RHODA *goes to the inner hall, and then comes out furtively, carrying a newspaper package.* CHRISTINE *emerges from the kitchen*]

CHRISTINE   What are you doing?

RHODA   Nothing.

CHRISTINE   Is that for the incinerator?

RHODA   Yes.

CHRISTINE   What is it?

RHODA   Some things you told me to throw away.

CHRISTINE   Let me see what's in the package.

RHODA   No.

CHRISTINE   Let me see it!
               [*She tries to take the bundle from a sullen Rhoda.* RHODA *suddenly snatches it back and tries to run.* CHRISTINE *holds on determinedly, and* RHODA *begins to bite and kick like a little animal. The package tears, revealing Rhoda's shoes.* CHRISTINE *wrests the bundle*]

*away, and pushes Rhoda violently from her, so that
she falls into a chair, staring at her mother with cold,
fixed hatred*]
You hit him with one of the shoes, didn't you? Tell me!
Tell me the truth! You hit him with those shoes! That's
how those half-moon marks got on his forehead and
hands! Answer me! Answer me!

RHODA   I hit him with the shoes! I had to hit him with the shoes,
             mother! What else could I do?

CHRISTINE   Do you know that you murdered him?

RHODA   It was his fault! If he'd given me the medal like I told
             him to I wouldn't have hit him!

             [*She begins to cry, pressing her forehead against table*]

CHRISTINE   Tell me what happened. I want the truth this time. Start
             from the beginning and tell me how it happened. I
             know you killed him, so there's no sense in lying again.

RHODA   [*Throwing herself into her mother's arms*] I can't,
             mother! I can't tell you!

CHRISTINE   [*Shaking Rhoda*] I'm waiting for your answer! Tell me.
             I must know now!

RHODA   He wouldn't give me the medal like I told him to, that's
             all. So then he ran away from me and hid on the wharf,
             but I found him there and told him I'd hit him with my
             shoe if he didn't give me the medal. He shook his head
             and said, "No," so I hit him the first time and then he
             took off the medal and gave it to me.

CHRISTINE   What happened then?

RHODA   Well, he tried to run away, so I hit him with the shoe
             again. He kept crying and making a noise, and I was
             afraid somebody would hear him. So I kept on hitting
             him, mother. I hit him harder this time, and he fell in
             the water.

CHRISTINE   Oh, my God, my God! What are we going to do, what
             are we going to do?

RHODA   [*Coquettishly*] Oh, I've got the prettiest mother! I've
             got the nicest mother! That's what I tell everybody! I
             say, "I've got the sweetest—"

CHRISTINE   How did the bruises get on the back of his hands?

RHODA   He tried to pull himself back on the wharf after he fell
             in the water. I wouldn't have hit him any more only he
             kept saying he was going to tell on me. Mother, mother,
             please say you won't let them hurt me! Please!

CHRISTINE   [*Putting her arms around Rhoda*] Nobody will hurt you.
             I don't know what must be done now, but I promise
             you nobody will hurt you.

RHODA   I want to play the way we used to, mommy. Will you
             play with me? If I give you a basket of kisses what will
             you give me?

CHRISTINE   Please, please.

RHODA   Can't you give me the answer, mother? If I give you
             a basket of kisses—

CHRISTINE   Rhoda, go into your room and read. I must think what
             to do.—You must promise you won't tell anyone else
             what you've told me. Do you understand?

RHODA   [*With contempt*] Why would I tell and get killed?

CHRISTINE   What happened to old Mrs. Post in Baltimore? I know
             so much, another won't matter now.

RHODA   There was ice on the steps—and I slipped and fell
             against her, and—and that was all.

CHRISTINE   That was all?

RHODA   No. I slipped on purpose.

CHRISTINE   Take the shoes and put them in the incinerator! Hurry!
            Hurry, Rhoda! Put them in the incinerator! Burn them
            quickly!

            [RHODA *takes the bundle*]

RHODA   What will you do with the medal, mother?

CHRISTINE   I must think of something to do.

RHODA   You won't give it to Miss Fern?

CHRISTINE   No, I won't give it to Miss Fern.

            [RHODA *smiles and goes toward the door*]

                        CURTAIN

Act Two

SCENE 2

After breakfast in the apartment, the next morning. At rise the stage is empty and the phone ringing. Leroy enters the front door.

LEROY

Leroy.
[*He looks at phone, starts toward kitchen and decides to answer phone. Goes back and takes it off the hook and hangs up. He starts back toward the kitchen and the phone rings again.* RHODA *enters from the kitchen*]
You better answer that phone.

RHODA

[*At the phone*] Hello—no, Mr. Bravo isn't here. Yes, I could write down a number.—Yes, sir.—I'll tell him. Goodbye. [*To Leroy*] I found out about one lie that you told. There's no such thing as a "stick blood-hound."

LEROY

I'm not supposed to talk to little Miss Goody-goody.

RHODA

Then don't.

LEROY

Where's your mother?

RHODA

Upstairs.

LEROY

For your own sake, though, I'll tell you this much. There may not be any stick blood-hounds, but there's a stick. And you better find that stick before they do,

73

because it'll turn blue and then they'll fry you in the electric chair.

RHODA There wasn't any stick any more than there were stick blood-hounds.

LEROY You know the noise the electric chair makes? It goes z—z—z, and then you swivel all up the way bacon does when your mother's frying it.

RHODA Go empty the garbage. They don't put little girls in the electric chair.

LEROY They don't? They got a little blue chair for boys and a little pink one for girls. I just remembered something. Just the morning of the picnic I wiped off your shoes with the cleats on 'em. You used to go tap-tap-tap on the walk. How come you don't wear 'em any more?

RHODA You're silly. I never had a pair of shoes like that.

LEROY They used to go tap-tap when you walked and I didn't like it. I spilled water on 'em and I wiped 'em off.

RHODA They hurt my feet and I gave them away.

LEROY You know one thing? You didn't hit that boy with no stick. You hit him with them shoes. Ain't I right this time?

RHODA You're silly.

LEROY You think I'm silly because I said about the stick. All I was trying was to make you say "No, it wasn't no stick. It was my shoes." Because I knew what it was.

RHODA You lie all the time. All the time.

LEROY How come I've got those shoes then?

RHODA Where did you get them?

LEROY I came in and got them right out of your apartment.

RHODA   [*Looking at book*] It's just more lies. I burned those
                 shoes. I put them down the incinerator and burned
                 them. Nobody's got them.

LEROY   [*After a pause*] I don't say that wasn't smart. That was.
                 —Only suppose I heard something coming rattling
                 down the incinerator and I says to myself, "It sounds
                 to me like a pair of shoes with cleats." Oh, I'm not say-
                 ing you didn't burn 'em a little, but you didn't burn 'em
                 all up like you wanted to.

RHODA   [*Waits with a new frightening stillness and intensity*]
                 Yes?—

LEROY   Now listen to this and figure out which of us is the silly
                 one. I'm in the basement working, and I hear them
                 shoes come rattling down the pipe. I open the door
                 quick and there they is on top of the coals only smoking
                 the least little bit. I grab them out. Oh, they're scorched
                 some, but there's plenty left to turn blue and show
                 where the blood was. There's plenty left to put you in
                 the electric chair!

                 [*He laughs a foolish little laugh of triumph*]

RHODA   [*Calmly*] Give me those shoes back.

LEROY   Oh, no. I got them shoes hid where nobody but me can
                 find them.

RHODA   You'd better give me those shoes. They're mine. Give
                 them back to me.

LEROY   I'm not giving them shoes back to nobody, see?

RHODA   [*With cold fury*] You'd better give them back to me,
                 Leroy.

LEROY   [*Laughing*] I'm keeping them shoes until—
                 [*His laughter dies under her fixed, cold stare. He begins
                 to be afraid of her. He no longer wants to play this
                 game*]

Who said I had any shoes except mine?

RHODA   You did. You get them and give them back.

LEROY   Now, listen, Rhoda, I was just fooling and teasing you.
            I haven't got any shoes. I've got work to do.

            [*He starts out*]

RHODA   Give me back my shoes.

LEROY   I haven't got nobody's shoes. Don't you know when
            anybody's teasing you?

RHODA   Give them back!

LEROY   Go and practice your piano lesson! I haven't got 'em, I
            keep telling you.

RHODA   Will you bring them back!

LEROY   [*Looking in*] I was just fooling at first, but now I really
            believe you killed that little boy. I really believe you did
            kill him with your shoes.

RHODA   You've got them hid, but you'd better get them and
            bring them back here! Right here to me!

LEROY   [*Outside*] Quit talking loud. There's someone in the
            hall!

            [CHRISTINE *enters*]

CHRISTINE   What was Leroy saying to you?

RHODA   Nothing.

CHRISTINE   I heard you say, "Bring them back here!"

RHODA   He said he had my shoes.

LEROY   I got nobody's shoes but my own. There's a number for
            Mr. Bravo to call.

CHRISTINE   You may go, Leroy.

LEROY   Yes, ma'am.

            [*He exits*]

CHRISTINE   Daddy, there is a message for you.

BRAVO   [*Entering*] Thank you, sweetheart.

            [*He takes the phone and dials*]

MONICA   [*Entering*] Look what I have for you, Rhoda! Turquoise! And the garnet, too!

RHODA   Thank you, Aunt Monica.

BRAVO   Hello. Listen, Murry, I know I ran out on you but this was imperative. Just wouldn't wait.—When does it leave?—Yes, I've had breakfast. If I get a taxi now I could just make it.—Yes, I've never been on the rig. I'd like to see it. And remember I've never missed a deadline. Think nothing of it.
            [*He hangs up*]
            I'll be gone a couple of days, but I plan to make this my headquarters the next few weeks if I may—

MONICA   As long as you can stand us—

BRAVO   Rhoda.

RHODA   Yes, granddaddy.

BRAVO   You ought to patent your smile. It does unfair things to your elders. . . . I really have to go, dear. I'll pick up the taxi at the corner.
            [*He puts his arms around Christine*]
            You are the bright thing in my life, Christine. It was you I lived for. You I loved. No matter what happens I want you to remember that. Don't worry. It will come out well.

CHRISTINE   Come back soon.

BRAVO   I will, sweetheart.
             [*He kisses Christine briefly*]
             My bag's upstairs. Don't come along. It'll be quicker.

             [*He goes out*]

MONICA   What a trouper!
             [*There is a sound of ice cream bells*]
             Ah, the ice cream man!

RHODA   Mother, could I have a popsicle?

CHRISTINE   Yes. Take the money from my purse.
             [RHODA *runs into the kitchen, then, coming out, stops
             to pick up matches as she passes the stove*]
             It is hot today.

MONICA   Yes, the streets seem deserted.

CHRISTINE   Rhoda, what have you got those for?

RHODA   I guess I just wasn't thinking.

CHRISTINE   I'll take them, please.

             [*She takes the matches and goes into the kitchen.* RHODA
             picks up another box and runs out. CHRISTINE *re-enters*]

MONICA   You won't mind too much if I'm nosey and ridiculous,
             Christine. You haven't been yourself lately. It's as if
             something's dragging you down.

CHRISTINE   Oh, dear. Do I seem that way to others?

MONICA   You mean you feel it?

CHRISTINE   Yes.

MONICA   Do you take vitamins regularly?

CHRISTINE   No.

MONICA   You should. That's one of the things we know. I have
          an awfully good combination, and I'll bring some down
          if I may.— And now you must really forgive me. Have
          you and Kenneth come to a parting of the ways? Is his
          secretary more to him than an expert on politics? Does
          she make a nest for him among the office buildings?

CHRISTINE   It's nothing like that, Monica. I wish I were as sure of
             other things as I am of Kenneth.

MONICA   Then do you suspect some disease—something like
          cancer, for example? If you do, we must face it and do
          everything that can be done. And a lot can be.

CHRISTINE   I'm perfectly healthy as far as I know.

MONICA   Do you sleep enough?

CHRISTINE   Well, no. Not always.

MONICA   You must have some sleeping pills. That much we can
          do. And now I won't bully you any more, Christine.
          I'm only going to say that I love you truly and deeply,
          my dear, as though you were my own; in fact Emory
          feels the same way about you, but I needn't tell you
          that, for you know it already.
          [CHRISTINE *puts her head down on the table and sobs*]
          Tell me what it is, dear. You can trust me.
          [CHRISTINE *gets up blindly, puts her arms around
          Monica, and weeps without restraint*]
          Dear, dear Christine. You'll feel better now. Perhaps
          you can get some sleep.

          [*The doorbell rings, and* CHRISTINE *stirs herself slowly
          to answer it*]

MONICA   Damn, I'll get rid of whatever—

          [*She goes to the door and opens it.* MRS. DAIGLE *stands
          in the doorway*]

MRS. DAIGLE   Well, Mrs. Breedlove. Hi. You don't want me here, and
               I don't want to be here, but I can't stay away, so I got
               a little drunk and came over. Excuse it, please.

MONICA   You're very welcome.

                [But the words come hard]

MRS. DAIGLE   Like a skunk, I know. Mrs. Breedlove knows every-
                body. Knows even me.

CHRISTINE   How are you, Mrs. Daigle?

MRS. DAIGLE   I'm half seas over, as the fellow—I just want to talk to
                your little girl. She was one of the last to see my Claude
                alive.

CHRISTINE   Yes, I know.

MRS. DAIGLE   Where do you keep the perfect little lady that was the
                last to see Claude? I thought I'd just hold her in my arms
                and we'd have a nice talk and maybe she'd remember
                something. Any little thing.

CHRISTINE   She's out playing.

MRS. DAIGLE   I'm just unfortunate, that's all. Drunk and unfortunate.
                Only she was right outside when I came by, ladies and
                gentlemen.

CHRISTINE   *[Going to the window]* She isn't there now. I don't see
                her.

                [But she couldn't, for her life, call Rhoda]

MRS. DAIGLE   She's a perfect little lady, never gives any trouble, that's
                what I heard. Have you got anything to drink in the
                house? Anything at all. I'm not the fussy type. I prefer
                bourbon and water but anything will do.
                *[*CHRISTINE *goes to kitchen and wheels out the bar]*
                Oh, ain't we swank? Really Plaza and Astor!
                *[*MRS. DAIGLE *pours herself a straight drink and downs
                it at a gulp, then takes a taste of water]*
                What I came here for was to have a little talk with
                Rhoda, because she knows something. I've called Miss
                Fern on the telephone a dozen times, but she just gives

me the brush-off.
[*She sits rather clumsily*]
She knows something, all right.

CHRISTINE   Are you comfortable there?

MRS. DAIGLE   I'm not intoxicated in the slightest degree. Kindly don't talk down to me, Mrs. Penmark. I've been through enough, without that.

[*The door opens and* RHODA *enters, delicately eating her popsicle*]

RHODA   I brought back change, mother.

CHRISTINE   Very well. Mrs. Daigle wants to see you.

MRS. DAIGLE   So this is your little girl? Claude spoke of you so often, and in such high terms. You were one of his dearest friends, I'm sure. He said you were so bright in school. So you're Rhoda.

RHODA   Yes.

MRS. DAIGLE   Come let me look at you, Rhoda. Now how about giving your Aunt Hortense a big kiss?
[RHODA *gives her popsicle to Monica and goes dutifully to be kissed*]
You were with Claude when he had his accident, weren't you dear? You're the little girl who was so sure she was going to win the penmanship medal, and worked so hard. But you didn't win it after all, did you, darling? Claude won the medal, didn't he? Now tell me this: would you say he won it fair and square or he cheated? These things are so important to me now he's dead. Would you say it was fair Claude had the medal? Because if it was fair why did you go after him for it?

RHODA   I want my popsicle.

MONICA   Rhoda, if you're going shopping with me, you'll have to come now. Mr. Pageson is going to show us his collection.

MRS. DAIGLE Right now?

MONICA We're a little late as it is. Bring your popsicle, Rhoda. You can wash upstairs.

[MONICA *disengages Rhoda from Mrs. Daigle and ushers her out of the room*]

MRS. DAIGLE Well, I must say!

CHRISTINE They do have an appointment.

MRS. DAIGLE I'm sure they do, practically sure. Of course, I didn't know Rhoda had all these social obligations. I thought she was like any little girl that stayed home and minded her mother, and didn't go traipsing all over town with important appointments. I'm sorry I interfered with Rhoda's social life. I'm sorry, Christine, and I offer my deepest apologies. I'll apologize to Rhoda too when I can have an interview with her.

CHRISTINE You haven't interfered at all.

[*The telephone rings.* CHRISTINE *answers it*]

MRS. DAIGLE I wasn't going to contaminate Rhoda in the slightest degree, I assure you.

CHRISTINE [*On the phone*] Hello. Yes, Mr. Daigle. Yes, she's here. Not at all.

[*She hangs up*]

MRS. DAIGLE Did you tell him I was drinking and making a spectacle of myself? Did you tell him to call the patrol wagon?

CHRISTINE You heard what I said. I said only that you were here. Your husband said he was in the drugstore on the corner.

MRS. DAIGLE I was just going to hold her in my arms and ask her a few simple questions.

CHRISTINE   Perhaps another time would be better.

MRS. DAIGLE   You think because I'm lit, but I'm not lit in the slightest
               degree, I assure you. But Rhoda knows more than she's
               told anybody, if you'll pardon me for being presump-
               tuous. I talked to that guard, remember. It was a long
               interesting conversation, and he said he saw Rhoda on
               the wharf just before Claude was found among the
               pilings. She knows something she hasn't told, all right.
               I know what you're thinking. You're thinking, "How
               can I get rid of this pest?" You may fool some with that
               mealy mouth, but you look like "Ned in the primer"
               to me.

CHRISTINE   Then perhaps you'd better not come here again.

MRS. DAIGLE   I wouldn't come here again for a million dollars laid
               out in a line! I wouldn't have come this time if I'd
               known about Rhoda's social obligations.
               [She pours herself another drink]
               I won't wait for Mr. Daigle. I'll go home by myself. I
               know where I'm not wanted, and I'm not wanted in a
               place where people have all these social obligations, if
               you get what I mean. You're looking sort of sick and
               sloppy. Come over to my house and I'll give you a free
               beauty treatment if you're pressed for ready cash. It
               won't cost you a nickel.

               [The doorbell rings and CHRISTINE opens the door. MR.
               DAIGLE is there]

MR. DAIGLE   Thank you, Mrs. Penmark. Come, Hortense, it's time
               to go home.

MRS. DAIGLE   Oh, my God, oh, my God, it's time to go home!
               [She embraces Christine at the door, resting her head on
               Christine's shoulder]
               Christine, you know something! You know something,
               and you won't tell me!

               [The DAIGLES go out. CHRISTINE stands for a moment,
               thinking, then goes to the phone and dials the operator]

CHRISTINE   [*Into the phone*] Operator, I want to call Washington, D. C.
[*She covers the speaker*]
Kenneth, darling, Kenneth, my dear love, what can I say to you? That our daughter is a——
[*She speaks into the phone*]
Never mind, then. No, cancel it.

[*She hangs up*]

[*The door opens and* MONICA *comes in, looks quickly around*]

MONICA   Good, she's gone. Sweet, I know I shouldn't take things into my all too capable hands, but I couldn't let her paw Rhoda any longer.

CHRISTINE   Mr. Daigle came for her.

MONICA   And I fear I've loosened discipline just a little. I let Rhoda go down for another popsicle.

CHRISTINE   Did she want a second? That's most unusual.

MONICA   She seemed quite eager. And since she's not one of these fat and self-indulgent little blobs I doubt that it can do any harm.—By the way, here are the vitamins and the sleep-capsules, both plainly marked.

CHRISTINE   Thank you, Monica. I'll keep them separate.

MONICA   Emory called while I was upstairs. He's coming by with Reggie Tasker to store some fishing equipment they bought this morning, so I'll get lunch for them. Wouldn't you like to run up and eat with us—you and Rhoda both?

CHRISTINE   Monica—I'd—I'd rather not, really.

MONICA   You poor girl, I do bully you, and I promised not to!

A VOICE   [*Off-stage*] Fire! Fire!

CHRISTINE   What was that?

MONICA   It sounded a little like somebody shouting, "Fire! Fire!"
              It sounded near-by.

              [*Other voices are now heard shouting, this time much
              nearer, and they are definitely crying "fire"*]

EMORY   [*Off-stage*] Fire! Fire!

TASKER   [*Off-stage*] Fire! Emory! This way!

              [RHODA *comes in. She has finished her second popsicle,
              and goes calmly to the den*]

CHRISTINE   Rhoda, who was shouting?

RHODA   I don't know, mother.

CHRISTINE   It sounds as if there were a fire!

RHODA   I don't think so, mother.

              [*She goes to den, closes door, and begins to play "Clair
              de Lune"*]

TASKER   [*Outside*] Fire! Fire!

EMORY   [*Outside*] Fire! Fire! The garage door!

              [*There is a rush of feet off-stage, and other voices add
              to the calling*]

VOICES   [*Outside*] Break the door down! Is anybody in there?
              Fire! Fire! That's Leroy's door! Break it down! Fire! I
              can hear him! Break it down! Break it down!

              [*There is a sudden ragged crash below, as if a door were
              split from top to bottom, and a man's screaming, as if
              he were in extreme pain*]

THE MAN   [*Screaming unintelligibly*] I haven't got 'em! I wasn't
              gonna do nothing! I was just saying it to tease you! I

haven't got 'em, I never had 'em, I was just— Oh God, oh God!

MONICA   [*At the window*] There's a man on fire!

CHRISTINE   His clothes are burning! His hair is burning!

[*The piano continues to tinkle*]

MONICA   Emory's there—and Reggie!

[*There is a man's scream, then silence*]

CHRISTINE   It's too late! He fell just before he got to the pond! He's lying still!

[*She slips to her knees, half-fainting*]

MONICA   [*Trying to draw Christine from the window*] Whatever can be done will be done.

CHRISTINE   I should have known it was coming! I should have known! Why am I so blind?

MONICA   Thank God Rhoda was in the den playing the piano!

CHRISTINE   The fire was in the garage! Where Leroy was!

MONICA   There's nothing we can do.

CHRISTINE   This time I saw it! I saw it with my own eyes. Tell them to stop screaming! It won't help to scream!

MONICA   Christine, Christine! You aren't making sense!

CHRISTINE   Tell her to stop the piano—and stop the screaming—I can hear it still, the man is still screaming, Monica, still screaming, and the piano going on and on while he's dying in fire, screaming, screaming a man's scream! [*The doorbell rings*]
              I don't want to see anybody now.

MONICA   It's probably Emory and Reggie, dear.

[CHRISTINE *remains sobbing on the chair,* MONICA *goes to open the door*]

EMORY   [*At the door*] Everything all right?

MONICA   Come in.

[EMORY *and* TASKER *come in, coats off and somewhat disarranged from a sudden encounter with fire-fighting*]

EMORY   We thought you'd be here. It was just a little flare-up in the garage; it's out now, but I guess Leroy—

MONICA   Never mind—

CHRISTINE   You can say it. I know about Leroy—I saw him burning, I saw him run down the walk and die! Could there be any worse than that?

TASKER   I guess you did see the worst of it, Mrs. Penmark. What seems to have happened is that he fell asleep on a bed he'd made out of excelsior, out in the garage, and his cigarette set fire to the stuff.

EMORY   And excelsior burns like gasoline when it's dry.

[*A siren is heard approaching*]

MONICA   You'd better leave me alone with Christine for a minute.

TASKER   That will be the ambulance.

EMORY   We can take care of that.

[EMORY *and* TASKER *go out. The tune continues in the den*]

CHRISTINE   I can't bear it! I can't bear it! She's driving me mad! [*She leaps up and runs toward the den*] How can she play that tinkle now? Rhoda! Rhoda!

MONICA   What is it, Christine? What is it?

[*She catches Christine's shoulders and holds her*]

CHRISTINE   It's heartless; I can't bear it! I can't, I tell you! Rhoda! Rhoda! Will you stop that music!

[*But it continues*]

MONICA   Try to make sense, dear!

CHRISTINE   Rhoda! Rhoda! Stop that music!

[RHODA *comes out of the den, wide-eyed and innocent*]

RHODA   Is mommy sick, Monica?

CHRISTINE   Don't let me get my hands on her.

MONICA   Christine, she's only a child.

CHRISTINE   You didn't see it! You could look away and play the piano, but it happened!

MONICA   Christine. Please be sensible. What has she done?

CHRISTINE   It's not what she's done—it's what I've done.

RHODA   What does she mean, Monica?

MONICA   I don't know, Rhoda. She'd better have lunch upstairs with me, Christine. She'll stay till you're calmer.

CHRISTINE   Yes, take her.

[*She sinks into a chair, shivering*]

MONICA   Will you be all right?

CHRISTINE   Yes, I'm all right. Only the screaming goes on and on.

[*She covers her eyes*]

MONICA   We'll come down for you. Come, Rhoda.

[RHODA *takes Monica's hand and they go out.* CHRISTINE *still sits, shivering, and her voice drops to a moan*]

CHRISTINE   She killed him. And I love her.—Oh, my baby, my baby!

[*She puts her head in her arms and weeps silently*]

CURTAIN

Act Two

SCENE 3

After dinner in the apartment, the same day. Rhoda is on the couch, in pajamas, ready for bed. Christine is reading to her as in the third scene of Act One.

CHRISTINE   "Polly put one toe out from under the covers to find out how cold it was, and it was nipping cold. She remembered why she had wanted to wake up, and got out of bed very softly, shivering and pulling on her dress and her stockings. She had never seen a Christmas tree decorated and lighted the way they are at Christmas in houses where children have fathers and it isn't hard times. She had promised herself that she would see one." [CHRISTINE *pauses and looks at Rhoda*]

You have some new vitamins to take tonight.

RHODA   New ones?

CHRISTINE   Yes.

RHODA   Are those the vitamins?

CHRISTINE   Yes.

RHODA   May I see them please?

[CHRISTINE *gives Rhoda the bottle*]

CHRISTINE   Yes, of course. They're some that Monica sent down for us.

RHODA   Okay, mommy. I think Monica likes me.

CHRISTINE   I'm sure she does.

RHODA   Swallowing pills is just a trick.

CHRISTINE   You're very good at it.

RHODA   Do you love me, mommy?

CHRISTINE   Yes.

RHODA   Mommy, do you know about Leroy?

CHRISTINE   Yes.

RHODA   You told me to put my shoes in the incinerator, didn't you?

CHRISTINE   Yes.

RHODA   Did you do something with the medal?

CHRISTINE   I drove out to Benedict today to see Miss Fern. And then I made an excuse to go on the pier alone—and dropped the medal in the deep water there.

RHODA   Mommy, Leroy had my shoes, and he said he was going to give them to the police and then tell them about me—and they'd put me in the electric chair. So— I had to—

CHRISTINE   You don't need to say any more.

RHODA   Will you read more now?

CHRISTINE   Take these first.

   [*Giving her a number of pills*]

RHODA   So many?

CHRISTINE   They're a new kind. I'm to take them, too.

RHODA   [*Taking the pills*] I like apricot juice. It doesn't even
            need ice. Mommy, I took another box of matches, and
            I lit the excelsior and I locked the door. But it wasn't
            my fault, mommy. It was Leroy's fault. He shouldn't
            have said he'd tell the police about me and give them
            my shoes.

CHRISTINE   I know.

RHODA   There. That's all. Don't let them hurt me, mommy.

CHRISTINE   No, dear, I won't let them hurt you.
            [*She leans over and kisses Rhoda*]
            Good night.

RHODA   Good night, mommy. Now will you read to me?

CHRISTINE   [*Reading*] "When Polly was all dressed she found her
            shawl and crept very quietly out of the room and out the
            front door. The door creaked, and she waited and lis-
            tened, but nobody woke up. She closed the door carefully
            and looked at the bright moon and the shining, cold snow.
            The Carters must have a tree. They lived two blocks
            away, and if they left the curtains open you could look
            in and see it. If only there weren't any dogs. Polly
            walked carefully on the hard snow on the walk, keeping
            the warm shawl close around her. It was further than
            she remembered to the Carters' house, but she could
            see that there were lights in the windows. She came
            near it, only making a little creaking noise on the snow,
            and stood for a while in front of the house before she
            dared go near. Then she gathered all her courage and
            walked across the yard, her shoes sinking through the
            crust. The Christmas tree was right in the front win-
            dow, and the lights were on in the house, so she could
            see the fruits and bells and strings of popcorn and
            candy—and the silver star at the top."
            [CHRISTINE *pauses and looks at Rhoda. She makes no*

sign, and her breathing is deep and regular. CHRISTINE
lays down the book]
Rhoda, dear. Rhoda, dear—you are mine, and I carried
you, and I can't let them hurt you. I can't let them take
you away and shut you up. They'd put you in some kind
of institution. Nobody can save you from that unless I
save you. So sleep well, and dream well, my only child,
and the one I love. I shall sleep, too.

[*She gathers Rhoda up in her arms gently, and carries
her into the bedroom. After a moment she returns and
opens a drawer in a spice cabinet high on the wall, takes
out a bunch of keys and goes to the den. There is a
shot and the lights go out*]

CURTAIN

Act Two

SCENE 4

Morning, a few days later. The sun is shining in at the window and Monica enters from the kitchen with a coffee tray. She sets it down and turns toward the kitchen. Emory, Tasker, and Kenneth come in from the outer hall.

MONICA   I've made coffee if anybody wants it.

EMORY   That's a thought.

TASKER   I'm in favor.

MONICA   [*Coming from the kitchen with a plate of sandwiches*] Kenneth? Coffee?

KENNETH   No, thanks, Monica.
            [*He goes to the window, looks out*]
            Now I must face living without her. Somehow I could almost believe she was still with me till they lowered that coffin into the earth—and I knew I'd never see her face again. Now the earth is empty, and I'm empty.

EMORY   She's left all of us feeling pretty much the same way.

KENNETH   And why did she do it? Why, in God's name, did she do such a thing? She wasn't unhappy when I left! Monica, she was closer to you than anyone else lately; did she say anything—that was any kind of a reason?

MONICA   I've gone over and over everything she said, till I'm al-
            most distracted—and it just doesn't fit any pattern! And
            I've talked to everybody who knew her—and they're
            just incredulous and shocked. There seems to be no
            reason at all!

KENNETH   There was a reason. Christine didn't do things without
            a reason.—Her father died suddenly, you said?

TASKER   He'd had a series of attacks, and the news of Christine's
            death seems to have been too much for his heart.

EMORY   She had some worry or other and I think it was con-
            nected with her father.

TASKER   I think she brooded over the Daigle boy's death and
            about the death of Leroy.

MONICA   She was hysterical at the time of the fire, but that was
            understandable.

KENNETH   [*To Monica*] When it happened how did you find her?
            Did you hear the shot?

MONICA   Yes—we heard it—and ran down. She'd shot herself
            and given Rhoda a deadly dose of sleeping pills. She
            had obviously planned that they should die together.

KENNETH   Could she—could Christine have been insane?

TASKER   No. We can rule that out. I talked with her not long ago.
            She shuddered somewhat—at my murder cases—but
            her comments were completely level-headed.

EMORY   No, Christine wasn't crazy.

KENNETH   I don't know how I'll live. I don't know that I will.

EMORY   I guess nothing helps.

KENNETH   Nothing.—I don't think it's much good without Chris-
            tine. The army—and promotion—and—a career—it
            was Christine that kept me afloat—not any of that.

EMORY   She was a wonderful girl.

KENNETH   And she left me—crept away into the earth—and I
             don't know why!
             [*His voice breaks, and he chokes down an uncontrollable
             sob, then another and another*]
             I'm sorry.

MONICA   You cry if you feel like it. She was worth it.

KENNETH   She didn't want to live.

             [*The piano in the den is heard playing "Clair de Lune"*]

MONICA   Kenneth, you have a lot to be grateful for. If we hadn't
             heard the shot you'd have lost Rhoda too.
             [MONICA *goes to den, opens door and calls*]
             Rhoda.

             [RHODA *enters*]

RHODA   Did you like it, daddy? I played it for you.

KENNETH   Oh, Rhoda, my Rhoda, there's a little of Christine left!
             It's in your smile!

RHODA   I love you, daddy! What will you give me for a basket
             of kisses?

KENNETH   For a basket of kisses?
             [*He looks at Rhoda*]
             Oh, my darling—I'll give you a basket of hugs!

             [*His arms go round her*]

                           CURTAIN